THE BEEF LOVER'S GREAT GRILL BOOK

BARBARA GRUNES

CB
Contemporary Books
CHICAGO

Library of Congress Cataloging-in-Publication Data

Grunes, Barbara.
    The beef lover's great grill book : favorite recipes for hot and sizzlin' grilled beef—as well as pork, veal, lamb, game, and more / Barbara Grunes.
        p.   cm.
    Includes index.
    ISBN 0-8092-4173-0 (paper) : $8.95
    1. Barbecue cookery.   I. Title.
TX840.B3G78   1991
641.5'784—dc20
                                                                      90-24787
                                                                           CIP

Copyright © 1991 by Barbara Grunes
All rights reserved
Published by Contemporary Books, Inc.
180 North Michigan Avenue, Chicago, Illinois 60601
Manufactured in the United States of America
International Standard Book Number: 0-8092-4173-0

CONTENTS

Acknowledgments *iv*
Preface *v*
The Right Stuff *1*
Your Guide to Perfect Grilling *7*
Marinades *11*
Recipes:
  Beef *13*
  Pork *37*
  Veal *66*
  Lamb *82*
  Game: Venison and Buffalo *97*
  Smoked Meats *112*
  Sausage and Burgers *125*
  Ember Cooking *134*
  A Grill Breakfast *142*
Appendix: Mail-Order Sources of Ingredients and Equipment *145*
Index *147*

ACKNOWLEDGMENTS

National Livestock and Meat Board
444 North Michigan Avenue
Chicago, IL 60611

National Pork Producers Council
P.O. Box 10383
Des Moines, IA 50306

PREFACE

I'm a middle-aged food writer, food historian, and food spokesperson who, like so many Americans, needs to eat healthier. I've reconciled my blood cholesterol level with a lifelong love of red meat and a passion for exuberant entertaining. Here's how:

I eat meats with less fat, have only about 3 ounces of cooked meat at a time, and practice creative cooking.

Grilled meats with innovative sauces and accompaniments have become my favorite way to prepare the foods I love.

- Searing leaner meats quickly on the grill retains their natural juices. I've included a time chart in this book, but use it as a rule of thumb rather than an absolute. Total grilling time varies according to the distance of the food from the coals, the temperature of the coals, the thickness and temperature of the meat, the wind, and weather conditions.
- Marinades add flavor to lean meats. (Much of meat's flavor is carried in the fat.) This book contains a marinade chart. Mix and match ingredients to customize your grilling repertoire.
- Accompany grilled lean meat with the right stuff: fruits, vegetables, yogurt-based sauces, relishes, and creative side dishes that are low in fat and high in fiber and complex carbohydrates.

I love sharing the recipes in this book with my family and friends, and now I am delighted to share them with you. May we all enjoy them in good health.

THE RIGHT STUFF

What do we mean by "the right stuff"? The right stuff is "lean and less" but also "more and better." Meat is *the* best source of dietary iron, the nutrient most often deficient in American diets, especially for women and children. Meat is also an excellent source of zinc, vitamin B_{12}, and other essential nutrients. The protein in meat provides all of the essential amino acids needed to build and repair cell tissues. Daily food guides suggest an intake of 5 to 7 ounces of lean meat, poultry, fish, or meat alternatives each day for healthy people of all ages.

Lower fat consumption is recommended to reduce the risk of heart disease. We especially need to reduce saturated fat found in animal foods and tropical oils. The meat industry has responded by developing hybrids, new feeds, and quality control in cutting and grading meats, so Americans can enjoy more varieties of leaner meats. Some of the new cuts of beef, pork, and lamb are lower in cholesterol too. And leaner meat has fewer calories than meat with more fat.

The recipes in this book call for many healthful ingredients. I've substituted canola oil and reduced-calorie margarine for butter. Olive oil, a healthful monounsaturated oil, gives a distinct flavor to marinades and side dishes, but use vegetable oil if you prefer. Canola oil, such as the Puritan brand name, is particularly low in saturated fats. Because saturated fats should be limited and meat contains saturated fats, it's wise to choose oils, dressings, and spreads that contain unsaturated fats and "save" saturated fats for meats and cheese that provide vitamins and minerals.

My menus include heart-healthy, high-fiber fruits, vegetables, beans, and whole grains. Salt has usually been reduced or replaced by more interesting herbs, spices, vinegar, wine, and fruit juices. Salting uncooked meat draws out the juices, just like salting a cucumber! If you must reduce salt intake, omit salt in recipes.

ALL THE TRIMMING

Though a good butcher will sell you "the right stuff" already trimmed to perfection, be sure you have a sharp, thin-bladed boning knife on hand to tackle the job yourself if need be. Boneless chops that look attractive in their packages at the market's butcher shop may have a thick layer of fat at the sides or bottom, where you can't see it until you've opened the package. For the most healthful fare, remove all visible fat from each piece of meat before grilling. But be careful not to poke holes in the flesh; it could cause juices to seep out during cooking, rendering the meat dry and tough. Some of the fat inside the meat (marbling) will melt away over the coals. But shop for the leaner cuts recommended here.

Boneless meats absorb smoke and heat evenly for more efficient grilling.

Special-order meats may be cut to your specifications. Be sure to order cuts in the appropriate size for your grill. However, some meats are just meant to be cut thick, so don't skimp. Pork chops are one meat that yields the most flavorful results when sliced thick.

THE RIGHT TOOLS

Assemble all equipment you need before you begin grilling. Just five minutes spent searching for your tongs can make the difference between delicious and dried-out meats. Adopt the Scouts' motto, "Be prepared."

To be an efficient grill cook, equip yourself with the following basics:

- a working grill
- charcoal
- a means to light the fuel
- special equipment such as a grill screen
- pot holders or insulated fireproof gloves
- long-handled tongs
- a platter
- a meat thermometer
- spray bottle for water
- a pan of cold water for sudden flare-ups

GRILLS GALORE

Whether your grill is an elegant electric grill or a humble hibachi, make sure you observe safety precautions during grilling. Place your grill away from doors, stairs, and high-traffic areas where it may be bumped. If it's a windy day, choose a spot where smoke won't blow into the cook's face or into the eating area.

If you plan to grill large cuts of meat, such as a butterflied leg of lamb, your grill must be big enough to support the weight of the meat. For small portions of meat, such as kabobs, you can get by with a smaller (and less expensive) unit. If you select a grill with a hood or cover, you'll have greater control of heat and smoking.

Hibachis make inexpensive and reliable grilling units. Made of heavy cast iron, hibachis have notched flanges to hold grilling racks at different heights above the coals. They are too small to accommodate large cuts of meat but will grill satay, kabobs, hot dogs, burgers, or chops for up to four people.

A *brazier* is a small, round grill up to 35 inches in diameter. Some braziers have lids or hoods; others are open. Some are on wheels, and others are stationary.

Barbecue kettles on wheels have a fitted lid. A kettle makes for efficient use of fuel and can be used to give a smoky flavor to food.

Electric or gas grills are convenient, as they may be heated without briquets. These grills may be installed as permanent fixtures on patios or be on wheels for portability. The design of an "automatic" grill is very important. If fat is not caught in a drip pan, you'll have greasy smoke.

The *water smoker* has a full container, a pan for water, a grill, and a sturdy cover. Smoke, the essential ingredient, is produced by the addition of presoaked wood shavings, chips, and twigs to the hot coals. Hickory, mesquite, and apple wood are the most popular. Food prepared in a smoker cooks for a long time over a slow fire. Check the manufacturer's directions for suggested cooking times.

A brazier may be purchased at many larger drugstores or discount stores, while more elaborate barbecue kettles are found at hardware, department, and cookware stores. Oriental grocery stores carry hibachis, as do most hardware stores. More elaborate grill wagons, smokers, and gas or electric grills are available in kitchen supply stores and by mail order.

GRIFFO-GRILL

One particularly effective piece of equipment for grilling meat is a stainless-steel wire rack called a Griffo-Grill. It fits directly on the grill and is so close-meshed that it provides maximum support for meat while allowing juices to drip through. The Griffo-Grill is an 11-inch square and will fit on almost any-size grill. It can be oiled lightly before each use to prevent meat from sticking to it. Sausages and burgers turn more easily on this grill, and spatulas are easily used. One of the ends is folded up to a 1-inch height to function as a spatula stop edge. The Griffo-Grill also prevents pieces of food on skewers from falling into the coals.

The Griffo-Grill is available in many hardware shops and supermarkets, as well as in gourmet cookware shops, but if you cannot find it in your area, you can send for it. The grill sells for $10.95, but if you order it by mail, enclose an extra $2 for shipping and handling. Send your name and address, written clearly, along with a request for the grill and a check for $12.95, to Griffo-Grill, 301 Oak St., Quincy, IL 62301. Your grill will arrive within two weeks.

A second Griffo-Grill, recently put on the market, has two handles and an ultra-heavy-duty frame and measures 12 by 16 inches. It sells for $27.95, which includes shipping.

HARD FACTS ABOUT CHARCOAL

There are two kinds of charcoal: hardwood charcoal made by burning hardwood until it is dry and porous and briquets made from compressed charred wood, paper, and/or sawdust.

Briquets are held together with petroleum-derived mastic that produces an acrid, damp smoke. The best briquets contain very little mastic. Choose briquets that smell faintly of burned wood. Avoid those that smell like motor oil.

The recipes in this book can be prepared successfully with briquets, but I highly recommend using hardwood charcoal.

Hardwood charcoal is made from live wood that is dried in a hot kiln until all that is left is pure carbon. It produces a clean, dry, intense heat that is well suited to grilling. It seals the pores of the meat quickly. Hardwood charcoal is favored by many top-notch chefs, who like the characteristic tang of wood smoke for their grilled dishes.

"Europeans never grill with anything but real wood," explains Don Hysko, president of People's Gourmet Woods. Hysko, whose father was Austrian, made frequent trips to Canada for hardwood charcoal before he began importing it to the United States in the early 1980s. People's Gourmet Woods now ships almost 4,000 bags a week to restaurateurs and consumers.

"It's possible to blend woods and create subtle flavors in smoke," Hysko says. Popular flavors range from the milder ash, sweet birch, chestnut, and walnut to the stronger oak, apple, and cherry. Alder and maple charcoals produce excellent medium-intense smoke. The more exotic woods, such as pecan, almond, lilac, and peach, are more expensive.

AROMATIC WOODS AND HERBS

Extra flavor may be added to grilled meats with aromatic woods or herbs. Simply soak two or three handfuls of chips or twigs from apple, cherry, hickory, maple, or oak and toss the drained, damp chips or twigs on the hot charcoal before grilling. The chips will smoke, adding wood flavor to the food. Hickory and oak go well with pungent barbecue sauces and marinades, while tender cuts of veal are best paired with fruit woods such as apple or cherry. Other possibilities for perfuming smokes include wine grapevines. People's Gourmet Woods will ship Pinot Noir or cabernet vines for grilling.

Add sprigs of fresh or dried herbs, soaked in water and drained, to the coals. Rosemary, tarragon, basil, oregano, sliced orange peels, whole cloves of garlic, and cinnamon sticks all impart an extra note of interest to foods cooked on the grill. Late summer or early fall herbs that are too woody for cooking are perfect for grilling.

"Feel free to experiment with mixing woods and herbs," Hysko says. "Sometimes I feel like an artist mixing my paints." Plan to use between 3 and 4 pounds of charcoal for each grilling session, less if there is leftover charcoal in the grill to use as a base for the fire. Hysko recommends using a fire chimney or an electric starter for real hardwood charcoal. "I use an electric starter because it's clean and doesn't have any chemicals in it," he says, "so why use a starter fluid made from all kinds of chemicals?"

Aromatic Woods

Apple
The sweetest and mildest of all woods, with a fruity aroma and an exotic, subtle flavor.

Cherry
An essence of ripened cherries with a slightly sweet bitterness.

Alder
Slightly sweet and very delicate.

Ash
Mild yet assertive, heavier than alder but still delicate.

Hickory
Hearty, heavy, rich, pungent, with a baconlike flavor.

Maple
Subtly sweet and mellow.

Mesquite
Hottest-burning wood, with a strong, sweet, honey and woodsy quality.

Oak
Smooth and mellow yet assertive (more so than ash).

Pecan
Sweet, nutty, and mellow, but burns cool.

Grapevine
Rich and fruity with a sweet wine flavor.

Oakies
Shavings from a red wine barrel interior; qualities of oak with a spicy, peppery undertone.

Seaweed
Tangy and fresh (needs to be sun-dried) enhancer.

Lilac
Floral and perfumy.

THE EXTRAS THAT MAKE GRILLING EASIER

Once you've got the basics on hand, consider adding the extras that make grilling easier. If your budget allows, a rotisserie spit makes it easy to roast meat inside a covered grill. Grill baskets with hinged lids simplify turning small medallions of pork tenderloin or other morsels. I recommend using the Griffo-Grill described earlier to grill vegetables, fruits, and small cuts of meats such as kabobs. Long-handled barbecue tools with handles made of an insulated material may be useful in retrieving meats about to be consumed by flames. Avoid wooden-handled implements, as they may char. For safety's sake, keep a water spray bottle on hand, as well as a pan of cold water. An extinguisher may be necessary if you're using lighter fluid.

Cookware that is extremely helpful includes the meat thermometer, especially important when gauging the doneness of lamb or pork. Everyone should invest in a good-quality meat thermometer, for it is a valuable aid in testing the doneness of meat. Both continual and instant thermometers are available, and the manufacturer's instructions that usually accompany each kind should be followed, but basically, insert the thermometer in the thickest area of the meat to a point where the tip is just past the center. The thermometer should not touch bone, fat, or gristle. When the thermometer reaches the desired temperature, remove meat from the grill, and remove the thermometer from the meat with a pot holder. Pastry brushes for dabbing on sauces are handy too. Skewers for kabobs may be elaborate metal ones or the inexpensive wooden (bamboo) skewers found in Asian groceries or restaurant supply houses. Always soak bamboo skewers in water and drain them before using them on the grill or cover the tips with aluminum foil. Fancy hot mitts, aprons, utensil racks, marinade and sauce holders, and other grill gear may be found in housewares stores and even some mail-order catalogs.

YOUR GUIDE TO PERFECT GRILLING

GRILLING METHODS

In the following chart and in every recipe in this book, we specify whether the meat (or other food) should be cooked by the direct or indirect grilling method.

For *direct-heat grilling*, after the coals have been lighted and are burning, evenly distribute them over the bottom of the grill. When they are ashen, place the grill rack over the coals, and set the food on it. Watch the food carefully as it can cook quickly and you do not want to overcook it. There is also the possibility of more flare-ups with direct grilling because of the rendered fat dripping onto the hot coals. Be sure to have a pan of water handy.

Use of the cover in direct-heat grilling: Usually you do not use the cover in direct grilling, but if you want to lower the temperature or obtain a slightly smoky flavor you can cover the grill. Cooking time will be slightly longer.

For *indirect-heat grilling* coals are piled three to four high on either side of a drip pan. A drip pan is a metal baking pan just larger than the area of the food that is to be grilled. There are two methods of preparing the briquets. The first is to set all the coals in a mound, ignite it, and then push half of the coals into two smaller mounds just large enough to fit the drip pan in the middle. The second is to place two mounds of briquets on either side of the drip pan and ignite both sides. Set the food on the grill rack placed over the pan so that the rendered fat and other liquid will not fall on the ashen coals and cause flare-ups. Just before grilling, when the coals are ashen, fill the drip pan halfway up with water. Cover and grill. This method helps keep the food moist and is a somewhat slower method of grilling.

Use of the cover in indirect heat grilling: The cover is most often used with the indirect-grilling method. Covering the grill gives the meat a somewhat smoky taste and it cooks at a lower temperature.

GRILLING HINTS

- When you're shopping, take your time. Read labels and select low-fat, low-cholesterol ingredients. Choose oils that are high in polyunsaturates and mono-unsaturates and low in saturated fats.
- Make friends with your butcher. Ask him to trim fat from meat. Always trim off any visible fat.

MEAT GRILLING GUIDE

BEEF GRILLING GUIDE			
Beef Cuts	Temperature of Coals	Direct Grilling	Indirect Grilling
Flank steak (1½ pounds)	Medium-hot	Sear 2 minutes each side; grill 3 minutes; turn once	NA
Beef tenderloin (1½ pounds)	Medium	Sear 2 minutes each side; grill 8 minutes; turn once	NA
Beef tenderloin (1¼ pounds)	Medium	NA	Sear 2 minutes each side; grill about 10-12 minutes; turn once
Chuck steak (2-2½ pounds)	Medium	Sear 2 minutes each side; grill 16 minutes; turn after 8 minutes	NA
Top round (1½ pounds)	Medium	Sear 2 minutes each side; grill 12 minutes; turn after 6 minutes	NA
Kabobs	Medium	9-12 minutes; rotate every 3 minutes	NA
Sirloin steak (2 pounds)	Medium	Sear 1 minute each side; grill 10 minutes; turn once	NA
Rib-eye steak (6 to 7 ounces each)	Medium	Sear 2 minutes each side; grill 8 to 10 minutes; turn once	NA

LAMB GRILLING GUIDE			
Lamb Cuts	Temperature of Coals	Direct Grilling	Indirect Grilling
Loin chop (4½ ounces)	Medium-hot	Sear 1 minute each side; grill 6 minutes; turn once	NA
Kabobs (1-inch pieces)	Medium-hot	Grill 9 minutes; turn every 3 minutes	NA
Butterflied leg of lamb (4-5 pounds)	Medium-hot	Grill 45 minutes; turn every 15 minutes	NA

PORK GRILLING GUIDE			
Pork Cuts	Temperature of Coals	Direct Grilling	Indirect Grilling
Center-cut chops (¾ inch thick)	Medium-hot	Sear 1 minute each side; grill 3-6 minutes each side	Sear 1 minute each side; grill 5-7 minutes each side
Center-cut chops (1 inch thick)	Medium-hot	Sear 1 minute each side; grill 5-7 minutes	Sear 1 minute each side; grill about 8 minutes each side
Double-cut chops (1½ inches thick)	Medium-hot	Sear 2 minutes each side; grill 6 to 7 minutes each side	NA
Pork loin (1¾-2 pounds)	Medium-hot	Sear 2 minutes each side; grill 8 minutes each side; rotate during grilling (30-40 minutes total)	Sear 2 minutes each side; grill 10 minutes each side; rotate during grilling (about 40-60 minutes total)
Kabobs (1-inch pieces)	Medium-hot	9-12 minutes; rotate every 3 minutes	NA
Ham slices (¾ inch thick)	Medium-hot	8-10 minutes; turn once	NA

VEAL GRILLING GUIDE			
Veal Cuts	Temperature of Coals	Direct Grilling	Indirect Grilling
Kabobs (1½-inch pieces)	Medium	9-12 minutes; rotate every 3 minutes	NA
Veal loin chops (½ to ¾ inch thick)	Medium	Sear 1 minute each side; grill 4-6 minutes; turn once	Sear 1 minute each side; grill 9 minutes; turn once
Veal rib chops (¾ inch thick)	Medium	Sear 1 minute each side; grill 4-6 minutes; turn once	Sear 1 minute each side; grill 9 minutes; turn once
Veal cutlets (about ½ inch thick)	Medium	NA	Sear 1 minute each side; grill 2 minutes each side
Veal loin (3 pounds)	Medium	NA	Sear 1 minute each side; grill 12-15 minutes (per pound); rotate every 5 minutes

- Use low-sodium soy sauce if you are trying to limit your salt intake.
- Grind your own meats with a food processor fitted with the steel blade. Select meat yourself and trim off excess fat. This ensures high-quality, low-fat ground meat.
- To cut meat paper-thin, freeze it until the meat is firm but can still be pierced with a fork.
- Always defrost frozen meat in the refrigerator. Bacteria can multiply quickly at room temperature.
- Keep meat chilled until grilling time.
- Use freezer-weight plastic bags for marinating meats.
- To crush peppercorns, place them in a plastic bag, seal, and crush with a rolling pin.
- Go light on the salt before grilling as it draws out liquid.
- To grease the grill grate, use extra-virgin olive oil, vegetable oil, or vegetable oil spray. This should be done when the grill is cold or away from hot coals.
- Carry charcoal in newspaper or in a washed and dried cardboard milk carton.
- Allow 20 to 30 minutes for the charcoal to become ready for grilling.
- Allow charcoals to become ashen ("ember-white") before placing food on the grill.
- Stir-fry on a grill over direct heat, with a heavy frying pan or wok. If you're using a wok, use the ring for stability.
- Have a bowl of water or a spray bottle on hand for flare-ups.
- Do not overcook lean meats as they become tough.
- To test meat for doneness, use a meat thermometer or remove a piece of the meat to a plate and cut into it.
- Allow meat to rest 5 to 10 minutes after it is removed from the grill.
- Slice meat against the grain.
- Remember to watch the grilling food carefully as it tends to cook quickly. If you see a thick piece of meat that's charring on the outside but is still raw on the inside, set it at the outer edge of the grill, away from the hottest coals.
- Freeze leftover grilled foods. Reheat in a microwave.

MARINADES

A marinade is a seasoned liquid used to impart flavor and/or tenderize meat. With the exception of game, few recipes in this book use marinades to tenderize meat. Lean meat, which does not have the more intense flavor of meat with more fat, lends itself to flavor-enhancing marinades. Marinades take just minutes to prepare, and once the meat is marinating, minimal attention is required until it is time to grill. Large cuts, such as butterflied leg of lamb, chuck steaks, and loins, should be turned occasionally during marinating so that all sides are coated evenly.

Marinades contain acid, and the process may take several hours. Always use a nonmetallic container that won't be affected by acid. Acid retards bacterial growth, but you should still refrigerate anything you're marinating for more than two hours. While the marinades contain oil, they do not add significantly to the fat or caloric value of meats after they are cooked, because most marinades are drained or the fat is grilled off the meat in cooking.

Don't be misled by the common misconception that more is better. Marinating for longer than 24 hours causes the meat fibers on the surface to break down, resulting in an unappealing, mushy texture. To avoid potential contamination, do not put cooked meat back into the container used for marinating, and don't pour leftover marinade over the cooked meat.

MARINADE CHART

In the following chart you'll find every marinade used in this book, listed by type and cut of meat. The chart is meant as a quick reference only; a marinade that imparts delicious flavor to the cut listed usually can be used for other cuts as well and even for other meats. Feel free to experiment and to create your own marinades. (See the Index for page numbers of the marinade recipes.)

MARINADE GUIDE

	Roasts	Steaks	Chops/Cutlets	Kabobs	Smoked
Beef	Red Wine Marinade I	Red Wine Marinade I Teriyaki Marinade Blueberry Marinade			
Pork	Citrus Marinade Green Peppercorn Marinade Sour Orange Marinade Hoisin Marinade and Brushing Sauce White Wine Marinade		Sofrito Sauce Citrus Marinade Honey-Mustard Marinade and Brushing Sauce	Five-Spice Marinade Whole-Grain Mustard Marinade Thai Marinade	Beer Marinade
Veal			Lemon-Sage Marinade	Whole-Grain Mustard Marinade	
Lamb	Red Wine Marinade I Rosemary Marinade			Mediterranean Marinade Anise-Orange Marinade	
Buffalo			Game Marinade		
Venison	Game Marinade	Mediterranean Marinade Red Wine Marinade II Game Marinade		Tarragon Marinade	Red Wine Marinade II Tomato Marinade

BEEF

Beef today is lower in fat and calories than ever before. It is likely to come from a steer that's both larger and leaner than its 1950s counterpart—the result of a 20-year effort to breed lean and tasty beef through improved feed nutrition and genetic research. Combined with closer trimming at the meat counter, that's good news for everyone who enjoys beef.

You don't *have* to pay premium prices for healthful beef. By choosing leaner cuts (round, sirloin, top loin, beef rib steak, flank steak, tenderloin, ground beef) and trimming visible fat, you can easily enjoy beef and stay within dietary guidelines.

Cutting larger cuts of meat—such as cutting chunks for kabobs from a chuck roast—is relatively easy to do and is an economical way of ensuring that each portion of beef you use is leaner.

Carpetbag Steak

For a special occasion, try this grilled steak recipe, which originated in Australia. Serve it with grilled kiwifruit (see box) and a salad. Warm Nectarine and Blueberry Compote (recipe follows) makes an ideal dessert.

OYSTER STUFFING
¼ cup extra-virgin olive oil
2 cloves garlic
¼ cup minced fresh parsley
1 cup bread crumbs
½ cup chopped fresh mushrooms
12 oysters, shucked
1 egg, slightly beaten
2 teaspoons grated lemon zest
¼ teaspoon salt
Freshly ground black pepper to taste

STEAK
1 flank steak, about 1½ pounds, trimmed of all fat

1. *Prepare the Oyster Stuffing:* Heat 1½ tablespoons of the olive oil in a frying pan. Add the garlic, parsley, and bread crumbs and fry over medium heat for 1 minute, stirring often. Remove the bread crumb mixture and set aside.
2. Add 1½ tablespoons more olive oil to the frying pan and heat over medium heat. Add the mushrooms and oysters and cook for 3 minutes, stirring often. Remove the oysters and mushrooms and set aside.
3. Pour the egg into a bowl and mix it with the lemon zest. Mix in the bread crumb mixture, oysters, and mushrooms. Toss ingredients together and season with salt and pepper.
4. *Stuff and Grill the Steak:* Prepare the grill for the direct method. Using a small, sharp knife, carefully cut a pocket in the thick part of the steak. Spoon the stuffing into the cavity. Secure the pocket shut with wooden toothpicks soaked in water for 10 minutes and drained. When the coals are ashen, brush the steaks with the remaining olive oil and place on the oiled grate. Sear 1 to 2 minutes each side and grill for 3 to 4 minutes on each side.
5. Cut the steak into individual serving pieces and serve hot.

Makes 5 to 6 Servings

Warm Nectarine and Blueberry Compote

4 cups chopped ripe nectarines
¼ to ½ cup sugar
1 cup fresh ripe blueberries
1 teaspoon grated lemon zest
½ teaspoon almond extract

1. Puree 3 cups of the nectarines in a food processor fitted with the steel blade or in a blender. Combine with sugar and spoon into a saucepan. Bring the puree to a boil over low heat, stirring often.

2. Remove the pan from the heat and add the zest and extract. Let sit until warm. Add the remaining nectarines and the blueberries. Serve warm over angel food cake.

Makes 5 Cups

GRILLED KIWIFRUIT
Cut kiwifruit in half lengthwise, place cut side down on a greased grill rack, and cook for 2 minutes.

Flank Steak with Tarragon-Almond Sauce

Serve this marinated flank steak with grilled zucchini spears (see Index).

Red Wine Marinade I (see Index)
1 to 1¼ pounds flank steak, trimmed of all fat

TARRAGON-ALMOND SAUCE
3 tablespoons extra-virgin olive oil
3 medium shallots, minced
2 cloves garlic, minced
2 teaspoons sugar
2 tablespoons tarragon vinegar (see box)
¾ cup tomato puree
¾ cup ground blanched almonds
¼ teaspoon salt
¼ teaspoon dried tarragon
⅛ teaspoon freshly ground pepper

½ cup fresh tarragon, soaked in cold water
    for 10 minutes and drained
2 tablespoons extra-virgin olive oil

1. *Prepare the Marinade:* Pour marinade into a large plastic bag. Add the steak and seal shut. Turn the bag several times to make sure all the meat surfaces touch the marinade. Marinate, refrigerated for 4 hours, turning occasionally.

2. *Prepare the Sauce:* Heat 3 tablespoons olive oil in a medium saucepan. Add the shallots and garlic and sauté over medium heat for 3 to 4 minutes or until tender, stirring often, making sure they don't brown. Add the sugar, vinegar, tomato puree, and ground almonds and combine. Simmer the sauce for 4 to 5 minutes. Season with salt, tarragon, and pepper; set aside.

3. *Grill the Steak:* Prepare the grill for the direct method. When the coals are ashen, sprinkle them with the fresh tarragon. Drain the steak, brush it with 2 tablespoons olive oil, and place it on the oiled grate. Cook for 2 minutes on each side, then continue grilling until the steak is done to your taste. (I prefer it slightly pink in the center, which will take about 8 more minutes for grilling.)

4. Place the meat on a platter and let it rest for 5 minutes. Meanwhile, reheat the sauce. Slice the steak into thin strips across the grain, drizzle with Tarragon-Almond Sauce, and serve hot.

Makes 4 Servings

Ember-Cooked Potatoes

6 large baking-type potatoes
Heavy-duty aluminum foil
3 tablespoons margarine

    1. Wash the potatoes and prick each one several times with the tines of a fork.

    2. Cut a piece of aluminum foil large enough to cover each potato generously. Place each potato in the center of a piece of foil and seal.

    3. Arrange the potato packets on the embers, avoiding the edge of the grill. Cover and cook for 45 minutes or until the potatoes are soft. Rotate the potatoes every 15 minutes until cooked.

    4. When the potatoes are done, remove them from the grill and unwrap and discard the foil. Cut a horizontal slash in each potato and serve hot. They can be garnished with margarine or low-fat yogurt and chopped green onions.

Makes 6 Servings

TARRAGON VINEGAR

Wash and pat dry with paper toweling 2 to $2\frac{1}{4}$ cups fresh tarragon leaves. Crumble the leaves and add them to 2 cups cider vinegar. Refrigerate for 2 weeks, strain, and pour the vinegar into a sterilized jar. Yields 2 cups.

Stuffed Flank Steak

This Argentinean dish is excellent when served either hot or cold on a buffet. The following recipe for rolled and stuffed flank steak has been adapted for the grill. Serve Raspberry Whip (recipe follows) for dessert.

STEAK
2 to 2¼ pounds flank steak, trimmed of all fat, with a 5-inch pocket cut in steak (you can ask your butcher to do this)

RED WINE MARINADE I
½ cup red wine vinegar
½ cup canola oil
2 cloves garlic, minced
¼ teaspoon freshly ground pepper
¼ cup minced fresh parsley
½ teaspoon dried thyme

STUFFING
¼ pound fresh spinach, washed, drained, and trimmed
1 carrot, sliced into rounds and cooked
2 hard-cooked eggs, peeled*
1 medium onion, chopped
1 cup coarse fresh bread crumbs
½ teaspoon salt
⅓ cup minced fresh parsley
½ teaspoon dried chili pequín, crumbled

1. Place a sheet of waxed paper over the steak and pound with kitchen mallet, until meat is uniform in thickness.

2. *Prepare the Marinade:* Combine the marinade ingredients and pour into a large plastic bag. Set the bag in a tray and add the flank steak. Secure the bag shut with a twist seal. Turn the bag several times to make sure all the meat surfaces touch the marinade. Marinate, refrigerated, 4 to 6 hours, turning the bag occasionally.

---

*Those restricting their cholesterol intake can either omit the eggs altogether or use only the whites.

3. *Prepare the Stuffing:* Remove the flank steak from the marinade and pat it dry. Arrange a layer of spinach in the pocket. Sprinkle the spinach with carrots. Set the eggs in the pocket. Toss the onion with the crumbs, salt, parsley, and chili. Stuff the mixture between the eggs. Add the remaining spinach. If there is room, seal the pocket with 8-inch wooden skewers soaked in cold water for 20 minutes and drained.

4. *Grill the Steak:* Prepare the grill for the indirect method. When the coals are ashen, place the meat on the oiled grate. Grill for 2 minutes on each side. Continue grilling until done to taste, about 4 minutes per side.

5. Remove the steak from the grill, place it on a platter, and let it cool for 5 minutes. Cut ½-inch slices, arrange the slices on a platter, and set on a buffet.

Makes 8 Servings

Raspberry Whip

My friend Robert Rusinko was the pastry chef at the 95th Restaurant at the top of the John Hancock Building in Chicago. He has created some beautiful desserts that are on the lighter side.

1-ounce envelope unflavored gelatin
2¼ cups raspberry puree or juice
¼ to ½ cup sugar
½ cup Chambord or another ½ cup raspberry puree
Fresh raspberries and fresh mint sprigs for garnish

1. Soften the gelatin in ½ cup of puree by sprinkling it over the top of liquid.
2. Warm the remaining puree in a saucepan over medium heat. Add the sugar and stir to dissolve but do not boil.
3. Melt the gelatin mixture in a small saucepan over low heat, then combine it with the sugar/puree mixture. Stir in the Chambord or additional puree and combine. Remove the pan from the heat and chill the mixture by setting the pan over an ice bath and stirring until it has the consistency of egg whites.
4. Divide the mixture among six dessert glasses. Beat the remaining raspberry gel with an electric mixer until pale and frothy. Divide it evenly among the glasses and chill until firm. Garnish with some fresh raspberries and mint sprigs.

Makes 6 Servings

Beef Tenderloin with Ginger Duxelles

Tenderloin seems rich and luscious but is surprisingly low in fat and calories. According to the National Livestock and Meat Board, an average 3-ounce cooked, trimmed serving of beef tenderloin has about 179 calories and 8½ grams of fat. Accompaniments of Grilled Corn Pieces (see Index) and a salad complement this elegant entree.

TERIYAKI MARINADE
⅓ cup peanut or canola oil
⅓ cup dry white wine
⅓ cup low-sodium soy sauce
2 tablespoons freshly squeezed lemon juice
1 teaspoon ground ginger
½ teaspoon minced garlic
1 teaspoon grated orange zest

BEEF
1¼ pounds beef tenderloin, trimmed of all fat

GINGER DUXELLES
5 tablespoons reduced-calorie margarine
1 large onion, minced
4 shallots, minced
1 pound fresh mushrooms, minced
½ teaspoon grated fresh gingerroot
½ teaspoon salt
¼ teaspoon freshly ground pepper
¼ cup dry red wine
2 tablespoons brandy

1. *Prepare the Marinade:* Combine the marinade ingredients and pour into a large plastic bag. Add the beef and secure the bag shut with a twist seal. Turn the bag, making sure all the surfaces of the meat touch the marinade. Place the bag in a shallow tray and marinate the beef, refrigerated, for 4 to 6 hours, turning the bag occasionally.

2. *Prepare the Duxelles:* Heat the margarine in a large, heavy frying pan over medium heat. Add the onion, shallots, and mushrooms and sauté for 5 to 7 minutes, stirring often. Season with ginger, salt, and pepper. Mix in the wine and brandy and continue cooking until warm. Set the duxelles aside.

3. *Grill the Beef:* Prepare the grill for the indirect method. When the coals are ashen, place the drained meat on the oiled grate and sear by grilling for 2 minutes on each side. Continue grilling, covered, for 4 to 6 minutes on each side or until the meat is done to your taste (about 10 to 12 minutes per pound). While the meat is grilling, reheat the duxelles until warm.

4. Transfer the meat to a platter, cut it into four to six serving pieces, and serve with duxelles.

Makes 4 to 6 Servings

Beef Tenderloin with Chimichurri Brushing Sauce

"The gauchos, or Argentina's cowboys, mark major events with a calf roast," says Lysette Davison, M.D., of Glencoe, Illinois. "The calf is butterflied and tied to a spit for roasting. Perhaps the best example of Argentina's love of grilling is the traditional parrillada, *a Sunday meal that is cooked on the grill in its entirety. A typical* parrillada *begins with chorizo sausage. Argentina's chorizo resembles the French* saucisson à l'ail *as it has no cumin but plenty of garlic and red pepper flakes. Try the following recipe for* chimichurri, *a spicy condiment served with special Sunday beef tenderloin."*

3 bunches parsley, washed and stemmed
8 large cloves garlic, peeled
¼ cup extra-virgin olive oil
Red pepper flakes to taste
Giardiniera peppers to taste
Olive oil
1¼ to 1½ pounds beef tenderloin, trimmed of all fat

1. *Prepare the Brushing Sauce:* Mix the parsley, garlic, extra-virgin olive oil, and red pepper flakes in a food processor fitted with the steel blade. Process to a thick paste. Add a scoop of giardiniera peppers to taste. Place the brushing sauce in a large glass bottle or jar and cover with a layer of olive oil. Before serving, shake well and brush seasoned oil over meat.

2. *Grill the Beef:* Prepare the grill for the direct method. When the coals are ashen, shake the sauce well and brush it on the meat. Place the meat on the oiled grate and sear by grilling for 2 minutes on each side. Brush on more sauce when you turn the meat. Continue grilling, covered, for 4 minutes on each side (about 10 to 12 minutes per pound), brushing with sauce when you turn the meat.

3. Transfer the meat to a platter, let it stand for 5 minutes, and slice thinly against the grain.

Makes 4 Servings

Boneless Rib-Eye Steak with Five-Herb Sauce

Five-Herb Sauce is adapted from an old German recipe. Serve this steak with Grilled Potato Skins or spinach noodles and Mixed Greens with Blueberry Vinegar Dressing (recipes follow).

HERB YOGURT SAUCE
2 cloves garlic, minced
1 teaspoon chopped fresh chives
1 teaspoon chopped fresh chervil
1 teaspoon chopped fresh watercress
1 teaspoon chopped fresh parsley
1 teaspoon chopped fresh dill
⅛ teaspoon ground mace
⅛ teaspoon salt
⅛ teaspoon freshly ground pepper
1 teaspoon prepared German mustard
3 tablespoons low-fat mayonnaise
2 cups plain low-fat yogurt

STEAK
3 6- to 7-ounce boneless rib-eye steaks, trimmed of all fat
3 cloves garlic, peeled and sliced in half

1. *Prepare the Sauce:* Combine the garlic, herbs, spices, and mustard in a bowl. Mix in the mayonnaise and yogurt. Refrigerate until serving time.

2. *Grill the Steak:* Prepare the grill for the direct method. When the coals are ashen, cut ¼- to ½-inch slashes on each side of the meat and insert a slice of garlic in each. Place the steaks on the oiled grate and sear by grilling for 1 to 2 minutes on each side. Continue grilling for 8 to 10 minutes, turning once, or until done to your taste. (I prefer it slightly pink in the center.)

3. Meanwhile, stir the sauce, taste, and adjust seasonings. Cut each steak in half. Place a piece of rib-eye steak on each of 6 plates and pass the cold sauce at the table.

Makes 6 Servings

Mixed Greens with Blueberry Vinegar Dressing

BLUEBERRY VINEGAR
2 cups frozen blueberries, defrosted and drained, or fresh
2 cups rice vinegar
2 tablespoons sugar

BLUEBERRY VINAIGRETTE
⅔ cup extra-virgin olive oil
⅓ cup Blueberry Vinegar
1 clove garlic, minced
¼ teaspoon salt
¼ teaspoon freshly ground pepper
¼ teaspoon dried thyme
1 teaspoon prepared coarse mustard
1 teaspoon sugar

GREENS
½ head romaine lettuce
1 head Bibb lettuce
1 medium red onion, sliced thin
½ teaspoon minced fresh basil
½ teaspoon minced fresh parsley
1 cup fresh blueberries (optional)

1. *Prepare the Vinegar:* Crush half of the blueberries and leave the remaining berries whole. Bring the rice vinegar to a boil in a saucepan over medium heat. Arrange the crushed and whole berries in a heavy ceramic bowl. Pour the vinegar over the berries. Cover with a double layer of cheesecloth and refrigerate for 3 days, stirring daily.

2. Discard 1 cup of berries and pour the remaining berries and vinegar into a saucepan. Stir in the sugar and bring the mixture to a boil over medium heat. Reduce the heat and simmer for 10 minutes.

3. Pour the vinegar into sterilized jars and seal according to the manufacturer's directions. Store in a cool, dark area. Or pour into a sterilized bottle and refrigerate. Use as needed.

4. *Prepare the Vinaigrette:* Combine the vinaigrette ingredients and whisk together. Transfer to a covered container and refrigerate for 1 hour. Stir before using.

5. *Prepare the Salad:* Wash and dry the lettuce; crisp it in the refrigerator until ready to serve. Toss the lettuce with the onions and herbs. Divide the salad among six chilled salad plates. Top with the vinaigrette and sprinkle with blueberries if desired.

Makes 6 Servings

Grilled Potato Skins

6 to 8 large baked or Ember-Cooked Potatoes (recipe follows)
3 tablespoons melted margarine
½ teaspoon garlic powder

1. Cut the potatoes in half lengthwise and scoop out the cooked potato, leaving ½ to ¼ inch of potato on the skin. Reserve the cooked potato for another use. Cut the potatoes lengthwise into quarters.
2. Brush the potatoes on all sides with melted margarine. Sprinkle with garlic powder.
3. Grill the potato skins on the oiled grate over ashen coals for 2 to 3 minutes on each side or to your taste. Transfer them to a serving dish and serve hot.

Makes 6 Servings

Chuck Steak with Szechwan Tangerine Brushing Sauce

Szechwan cuisine is characterized by highly distinctive flavors. It makes good use of native chili peppers, sesame, and black beans. Ingredients such as dried tangerine peel, five-spice seasoning, and fennel add to its character. Szechwan meat is often smoked with burning tea as an aromatic. Serve this steak with Oriental noodles or cellophane noodles cooked in beef stock and grilled vegetables.

Teriyaki Marinade (see Index)
1 2- to 2½-pound boneless chuck steak, trimmed of all fat

SZECHWAN TANGERINE BRUSHING SAUCE
¼ cup canola oil
½ teaspoon (or to taste) red pepper flakes
2 cloves garlic, minced
¾ teaspoon grated fresh gingerroot
2 tablespoons grated tangerine zest
1 large onion, sliced thin
2 teaspoons Oriental chili sauce
2 red or green bell peppers, seeded and cut into strips
2 tablespoons shredded tangerine zest

4 stems dried sage, tied together at one end (optional)

1. *Marinate the Beef:* Pour the marinade into a large plastic bag or shallow dish. Add the meat and secure the bag shut with a twist seal. Turn the bag several times so that all surfaces are touched by the marinade. Marinate, refrigerated, for 4 to 6 hours or overnight, turning occasionally.

2. *Prepare the Brushing Sauce:* While the meat is marinating, heat the oil in a wok or a heavy frying pan. Stir-fry the red pepper flakes, garlic, ginger, grated tangerine zest, and onion for about 45 seconds over medium to high heat. Stir in the chili sauce, bell pepper strips, shredded tangerine zest. Stir-fry for 2 minutes. Set the sauce aside.

3. *Grill the Beef:* Prepare the grill for the direct method. When the coals are ashen, drain the meat and place it on the oiled grate, reserving the marinade.

Sear the steak by grilling for 2 minutes on each side. Use the sage brush or a pastry brush to brush the steak with the marinade when you turn it. Continue cooking for 6 to 8 minutes on each side, or until the meat is cooked to your taste. It should be slightly pink on the inside when done.

4. Transfer the meat to a cutting board and let it rest for 5 minutes. Meanwhile, reheat the sauce. Slice the meat against the grain into thin pieces. Cover it with sauce and serve hot.

Makes 8 Servings

GRILLED ZUCCHINI SPEARS
Cut zucchini into spears and brush them with prepared low-calorie Italian salad dressing. Grill over ashen coals for 1 minute on each side.

Ann Hunt's Top Round with Rhubarb-Berry Sauce

Dried blueberries are available by mail order (see Appendix). For side dishes, try grilled squash and brown rice.

BLUEBERRY MARINADE
½ cup canola oil
½ cup dry red wine or Blueberry Vinegar (see Index)
½ cup dried blueberries or fresh or defrosted frozen
½ teaspoon ground cinnamon
½ teaspoon ground ginger

STEAK
1¼ to 1½ pounds top round steak

RHUBARB-BERRY SAUCE
1 1-pound package frozen rhubarb, defrosted
½ cup dried blueberries or defrosted frozen
¼ cup cider vinegar
5 tablespoons light brown sugar
½ teaspoon ground cinnamon
½ teaspoon salt
½ teaspoon dry mustard
¼ teaspoon ground mace
⅛ teaspoon ground cloves

3 to 4 cups cherry twigs, soaked in cold water for 30 minutes and drained (optional)

1. *Prepare the Marinade:* Combine the marinade ingredients and pour into a large plastic bag. Add the steak and secure the bag shut with a twist seal. Turn the bag several times so that all surfaces of the steak are coated with marinade. Place the bag in a shallow dish and marinate, refrigerated, for 4 to 6 hours or overnight, turning occasionally.

2. *Prepare the Sauce:* While the meat is marinating, blend the sauce ingredients in a saucepan over medium heat. Bring the sauce to a boil, reduce the heat, and simmer the sauce for 4 to 5 minutes, stirring often. Taste to adjust seasonings and set aside.

3. *Grill the Beef:* Prepare the grill for the direct method. When the coals are ashen, sprinkle the twigs over the coals and replace greased grate. Drain the meat, reserving the marinade. Place the meat on the oiled grate and sear for 2 minutes on each side. Continue grilling for 4 to 6 minutes on each side or until done to your taste. For medium, leave the meat pink in the center.

4. Transfer the meat to a platter and let it stand for 5 minutes. Meanwhile, reheat the sauce. Slice the meat into thin strips across the grain. Spoon the sauce around the meat and serve hot.

Makes 4 to 6 Servings

GRILLED ACORN SQUASH

Cut in half and discard seeds. Sprinkle cavity with light brown sugar mixed with cinnamon to taste. Wrap each half in foil and set directly on the coals. Cook about 35 minutes on embers, turning once or twice, until tender.

Lightly Grilled Steak Carpaccio

These melt-in-your-mouth, wafer-thin slices of beautifully seasoned beef will linger in your memory. Gazpacho and bulgur salad go nicely with Steak Carpaccio. Try Tequila Lime Sorbet (recipe follows) for dessert.

Red Wine Marinade I (see Index)

CINNAMON SAUCE
1 large shallot, minced
1 clove garlic, minced
½ teaspoon dried tarragon
½ teaspoon ground cinnamon
½ teaspoon sugar
¼ cup minced fresh parsley
¼ cup tarragon vinegar
½ cup extra-virgin olive oil

STEAK
1 pound boneless lean strip sirloin, trimmed of all fat
2 tablespoons crushed green peppercorns (see box)
1 tablespoon crushed black peppercorns (see box)
3 cups hickory chips, soaked in cold water for 30 minutes and drained
½ cup trimmed fresh parsley for garnish

1. *Marinate the Beef:* Pour the marinade into a large plastic bag. Add the steak and secure the bag shut with a twist seal. Turn the bag several times so that all surfaces of the meat touch the marinade. Marinate, refrigerated, 4 to 6 hours, turning occasionally.

2. *Prepare the Sauce:* Mix the shallots, garlic, tarragon, cinnamon, sugar, parsley, and vinegar in a bowl. Whisk in the oil, combining the ingredients. Set aside.

3. *Grill the Beef:* Prepare the grill for the direct method. Brush the steak with the sauce and press peppercorns into both sides of the meat. When the coals are ashen, sprinkle them with hickory chips. Arrange the steak on the oiled grate and sear by grilling for 2 minutes on each side.

4. Slice the meat paper-thin across the grain. Arrange the steak slices in a fan design on six plates. Spoon the dipping sauce over the meat and serve immediately, garnished with parsley sprigs.

Makes 6 Servings

Tequila Lime Sorbet

Tequila Lime Sorbet is wonderful as an intermezzo or as a refreshing end to a Mexican dinner. It was developed by Robert Rusinko, former pastry chef, 95th Restaurant, Chicago.

3½ cups water
1¾ cups sugar
2 tablespoons grated lime zest
1½ cups freshly squeezed lime juice
¼ cup vodka
½ cup gold tequila

1. Combine water, sugar, and zest in a saucepan. Bring to a boil and continue cooking for 2 minutes to make a syrup. Remove from heat and cool. Strain the zest from the syrup and combine the syrup with the juice, vodka, and tequila.
2. Transfer the mixture to a shallow dish and chill until very cold.
3. Pour the mixture into an ice cream freezer and freeze according to the manufacturer's instructions.

Makes 6 Servings

TO CRUSH PEPPERCORNS

Place peppercorns between two sheets of waxed paper or in a durable plastic bag and crush with a rolling pin using a repeated rolling motion.

Beef Kabobs with Balsamic Vinegar Brushing Sauce

Cutting your own kabobs is easy to do and is an economical way to ensure that each piece of beef you use is lean. Serve the kabobs over a bed of cooked barley.

BALSAMIC VINEGAR BRUSHING SAUCE
3 tablespoons extra-virgin olive oil
2 tablespoons balsamic vinegar
⅓ cup dry red wine
½ teaspoon dry mustard
½ teaspoon dried basil
¼ cup chopped cilantro

KABOBS
6 wooden skewers, soaked in cold water for 20 minutes and drained
1 pound lean beef tenderloin or other lean beef, trimmed of all fat and cut into 1-inch pieces
½ pound large fresh mushrooms, cleaned and trimmed
2 red bell peppers, seeded and cut into squares
6 small patty pan squash, cut in half

3 to 4 cups hickory chips *or* 1 cup torn fresh basil leaves soaked in cold water for 15 minutes and drained (optional)

1. Prepare the grill for the direct method.
2. *Prepare the Brushing Sauce:* Combine the sauce ingredients in a small bowl and set the bowl near the grill.
3. Thread each skewer alternately with beef, mushrooms, peppers, and squash. Brush with the sauce.
4. *Grill the Kabobs:* When the coals are ashen, replace the oiled grate or use an oiled grill screen. Place the kabobs on the grate or screen and grill for about 9 to 12 minutes, rotating them every 3 to 4 minutes and brushing them with sauce when you turn them. The meat should be done to just medium for the best results.

Makes 6 Servings

Warm Steak Salad with Ginger and Pepper Vinaigrette

This recipe was created by Alexander S. Dering, executive chef at Chicago's L'Escargot on Michigan, who advises, "Other types of meat may be used for this salad, such as flank steak, skirt steak, top round, etc. The important procedure is to slice the meat against the grain and very thin, so that it is not chewy. You may also marinate the meat for a longer period of time. Bon appétit!*"*

GINGER AND PEPPER VINAIGRETTE
1½ tablespoons minced fresh gingerroot
1½ tablespoons minced garlic
1 teaspoon cracked pepper
½ cup peanut oil
½ cup dark sesame oil
½ cup white rice vinegar
6 ounces soy sauce

BEEF
4 to 6 ounces boneless center-cut choice
   sirloin
2 tablespoons minced shallot
1 teaspoon minced fresh thyme
½ cup virgin olive oil
Salt and freshly ground pepper to taste

SALAD MIXTURE
¾ cup spinach leaves, cleaned and left
   whole
¾ cup curly endive, cut into 2-inch pieces
¾ cup mâche (lamb's lettuce), cleaned and
   left whole
1 head radicchio, 4 large, cup-shaped leaves
   left whole, the rest cut into 2-inch pieces
¾ cup Napa cabbage, cut into 2-inch pieces
1 cup carrots, julienned
1 cup snow peas, julienned

1. *Prepare the Vinaigrette:* Mix all vinaigrette ingredients together well and let stand for at least 24 hours. *Do not refrigerate.*

2. *Marinate the Meat:* Place the meat in a pan and add the shallots, thyme, and olive oil. Season lightly with salt and pepper and marinate, refrigerated, for at least 2 hours.

3. *Prepare the Salad Mixture:* Put the salad ingredients in a large bowl, cover with a damp towel, and refrigerate until needed.

4. Prepare the grill for the direct method. While the coals are heating, remove the salad mixture from the refrigerator and leave at room temperature.

5. *Grill the Meat:* When the coals are ashen, toss the salad mixture with the desired amount of vinaigrette (you will have more than you need for four salads) and divide among four serving plates. Garnish each plate with one radicchio cup and set aside. Remove the steaks from the marinade and place on the oiled grate. Sear on both sides for 2 minutes. Continue grilling for 8 to 10 minutes, turning once, until steak is pink in the center or until done to your taste.

6. Transfer the steak to a cutting surface, let it stand for 10 minutes, and slice very thin on the diagonal, across the grain. Place slices on top of each salad. Drizzle with the remaining vinaigrette or serve the vinaigrette on the side.

Makes 4 Servings

Hot Sliced Sirloin Steak on Salad with Yogurt Horseradish Sauce

A hot and cold combination with an intriguing combination of textures that is light and spicy at the same time.

YOGURT HORSERADISH SAUCE
2 cups plain low-fat yogurt
2 tablespoons (or to taste) prepared white horseradish
¼ cup minced fresh parsley

STEAK
1¾ to 2 pounds boneless sirloin steak, trimmed of visible fat
¼ teaspoon freshly ground black pepper
2 cloves garlic, minced

SALAD
2 heads red leaf lettuce, washed and dried
2 tomatoes, sliced thin
1 medium red onion, sliced thin
½ teaspoon salt
¼ teaspoon freshly ground pepper

1. *Prepare the Sauce:* Spoon the yogurt into a bowl and blend in the horseradish and parsley. Cover and refrigerate until needed. Stir before serving.
2. Prepare the grill for the direct method.
3. *Grill the Steak:* When the coals are ashen, sprinkle both sides of the meat with ¼ teaspoon pepper and the garlic. Place the steak on the oiled grate and sear for 1 minute on each side. Continue grilling for 5 minutes on each side, until the steak is pink in the center or until done to your taste.
4. Transfer the meat to a platter and let it stand for 10 minutes. Slice it thin, against the grain.
5. *Prepare the Salad:* Divide the lettuce leaves evenly among six to eight plates, add the tomato and onion slices, and sprinkle with the salt and ¼ teaspoon pepper. Arrange the meat slices over the salad and top with a dollop of Yogurt Horseradish Sauce. Pass extra sauce at the table.

Makes 6 to 8 Servings

PORK

America's appetite for "the other white meat" is increasing. Improvements in breeding and production technology have resulted in pork that is an average of 50 percent leaner than pork produced in the 1960s. Calorie-conscious consumers can eat pork fearlessly: a 3-ounce serving of loin contains fewer than 200 calories!

Following two years of research, the National Pork Producers Council recently introduced revised cooking recommendations. Most of today's popular fresh pork cuts are done and safe to eat at an internal temperature of 160°F. While some people may prefer pork well done, lean pork is juicier when cooked to medium. This reduced cooking temperature means quicker meal preparation for time-conscious cooks.

Pork Chops with Herb-Tomato Sauce and Whole-Wheat Pasta

Fresh tomato puree is best (see box), but canned can be used instead. Antipasto is the perfect accompaniment.

HERB-TOMATO SAUCE
1 tablespoon extra-virgin olive oil
3 cloves garlic, minced
2 medium onions, chopped
2 green bell peppers, seeded and chopped
¾ pound fresh mushrooms, cleaned, trimmed and sliced (if mushrooms are small, leave whole)
3 cups tomato puree or sauce
1½ teaspoons crumbled dried oregano
1½ teaspoons crumbled dried basil
1 teaspoon crumbled dried marjoram
1½ teaspoons fennel seeds
¼ teaspoon (or to taste) cayenne pepper
¼ teaspoon (or to taste) salt
⅓ cup water

1 pound no-yolk pasta, whole-wheat pasta, or other pasta of your choice
6 1-inch-thick pork chops, about 1¾ to 2 pounds total
2 tablespoons extra-virgin olive oil
6 bay leaves
½ cup dried fennel seeds, soaked in cold water for 10 minutes and drained

1. *Prepare the Sauce:* Heat 1 tablespoon olive oil in a saucepan. Add the garlic, onions, and peppers and sauté over medium heat for 4 to 5 minutes, stirring occasionally. Add the mushrooms and cook for 2 minutes. Stir in the tomato puree or sauce, oregano, basil, marjoram, fennel seeds, cayenne, salt, and water. Simmer the sauce for 10 minutes, stirring occasionally. Set the sauce aside.

2. *Prepare the Pasta:* Cook the pasta according to the package directions. Drain and set aside.

3. *Grill the Pork:* Prepare the grill for the direct method. Brush the pork chops with 2 tablespoons oil and press a bay leaf onto each chop. When the coals are ashen, sprinkle them with the drained fennel seeds. Place the chops on the oiled grate and sear for 1 minute on each side. Continue grilling for 6 to 8 minutes or until cooked to medium. Meanwhile, reheat the sauce.

4. To serve, refresh the pasta under hot water and divide the pasta among six plates. Remove the bay leaves from the chops and set a pork chop on top. Drizzle with sauce.

Makes 6 Servings

TO PUREE TOMATOES

Peel tomatoes by plunging them into a large pot of boiling water for about 10 seconds. Remove the tomatoes, drop into a bowl of ice water, and slip off the skins.

Squeeze the tomatoes gently to extract the seeds and juice, then put the pulp in a food processor fitted with the steel blade or in a blender. Process until a smooth puree results.

Pork with Mole

As the story goes, mole was created out of need. It seems one day, during Mexico's colonial period, an unexpected visitor came to call on the convent of Puebla. The sisters wanted to make a very special meal for the occasion. They adapted an Indian dish called mole *and served it with a turkey. Thus* mole poblano *was created. The sauce is a great success with pork and is easily made in the food processor. The sauce itself is a warm, reddish-brown color. Ingredients vary, but there is always a small amount of dark chocolate, which adds richness without sweetness. Mole is a perfect accompaniment for pork. Serve this recipe with warm tortillas, orange and red onion salad, and grilled tomatillos.*

MOLE SAUCE
2 tablespoons canola oil
4 ancho dried chilies, soaked in water for 20 minutes, seeds and stems discarded
½ cup ground almonds
1 medium onion, minced
1½ cups chicken stock
2 corn tortillas, crumbled
1 large tomato, peeled, seeded, and chopped
¼ cup dark raisins
½ teaspoon ground cinnamon
½ teaspoon salt
¼ teaspoon ground cloves
2 tablespoons sesame seeds
½ ounce semisweet chocolate, melted

PORK
4 1½-inch-thick boned center-cut pork chops

1. *Prepare the Sauce:* Heat the oil in a saucepan over medium heat. Add the chilies, almonds, and onions and sauté for 4 minutes, stirring often. Add the remaining ingredients except pork chops and simmer for 10 minutes. Cool the sauce and puree it in a food processor fitted with the steel blade or in a blender. Refrigerate until needed.

2. *Grill the Pork:* Prepare the grill for the direct method. When the coals are ashen, place the pork chops on the oiled grate and brush them lightly with mole sauce. Sear for 2 minutes on each side and continue grilling, covered, for 6 to 7 minutes. Brush the pork again, turn, and grill, covered, for 6 minutes or until done to taste. Do not overcook. (The chops can be cooked using the indirect method. Sear the chops and grill over a drip pan. They may take a few minutes longer to cook using this method.)

3. Remove the sauce from the refrigerator and reheat. Drizzle mole sauce onto individual plates and set a chop in the center of each.

Makes 4 Servings

Butterflied Pork Chops with Sofrito Sauce

Sofrito sauce is both Spanish and Caribbean. Our "light" Spanish version is perfect with pork chops. Serve this entree with rice, Hearts of Palm Salad with Walnut Oil Dressing (see Index), and Grilled Pineapple Slices (see Index).

SOFRITO SAUCE
3 tablespoons canola oil
1 large onion, sliced thin
3 cloves garlic, minced
1 small red bell pepper, seeded and chopped
3 large tomatoes, peeled, seeded, and chopped, *or* 3 cups drained canned tomatoes
½ teaspoon salt
¼ teaspoon paprika
¼ teaspoon dried oregano
¼ teaspoon freshly ground pepper
⅛ teaspoon saffron threads

PORK
4 butterflied pork chops, about 1¼ pounds total, trimmed of all fat
3 cups hickory chips, soaked in cold water for 30 minutes and drained

1. *Make the Sauce:* Heat the oil in a frying pan over medium heat. Add the onion, garlic, and bell pepper and sauté for 5 minutes, stirring often. Mix in the tomatoes, salt, paprika, oregano, pepper, and saffron. Continue cooking for 10 minutes or until the sauce thickens. Cool the sauce and puree it in a food processor fitted with the steel blade or in a blender. Set aside.

2. *Marinate the Pork:* Brush the pork chops with some of the sofrito sauce and place them, along with the sauce, in a large plastic bag. Secure with a twist seal and turn the bag so that all surfaces of the pork touch the sauce. Let stand at room temperature for 2 hours.

3. *Grill the Pork:* Prepare the grill for the direct method. When the coals are ashen, sprinkle the hickory chips over them and replace the oiled grate or use a grill rack. Arrange the pork chops, open side down, on the grate. Sear chops by grilling for 1 minute on each side. Continue grilling for 4 to 6 minutes. Brush with sofrito sauce, turn, and grill for 5 to 6 minutes longer. Chops are done when they are opaque in the center.

Makes 4 Servings

Pork Chops Brushed with Two-Pepper Jelly

Two-Pepper Jelly is a bright green, tangy, and yet not too hot jelly that makes a lovely gift. If you opt not to use the food coloring, the taste will be the same but the jelly will be lighter in color. These chops are good with salsa and warm tortillas. (Heat the tortillas, wrapped in foil, on the grill until warm.)

½ cup Two-Pepper Jelly (recipe follows)
4 ¾-inch-thick pork chops about 1½ pounds total, trimmed of all fat
3 cups mesquite chips, soaked in cold water for 30 minutes and drained
½ cup freshly squeezed orange juice

1. *Prepare the Jelly:* Spoon the jelly into a saucepan and mix in 1 tablespoon water. Cook over medium heat until melted, stirring often. Set aside.

2. *Grill the Pork:* Prepare the grill for the indirect method, placing the orange juice mixed with 1 cup of water in the drip pan. When the coals are ashen, brush the pork chops liberally on both sides with the melted jelly. Sprinkle the coals with the mesquite chips and place the chops on the oiled grate.

3. Sear the chops by grilling for 1 minute on each side. Continue grilling, covered, for 6 minutes. Turn the pork chops and continue grilling, covered, for 5 to 7 minutes or until done. Transfer the chops to a serving platter and serve hot.

Makes 4 Servings

Two-Pepper Jelly

When you're working with jalapeño peppers, remember to wear rubber gloves and avoid touching your eyes until you wash your hands. The cider vinegar produces a slightly tart, clear jelly.

> 1 large yellow or red bell pepper, seeded and sliced
> 5 large fresh jalapeño peppers, seeded and chopped
> 6 cups sugar
> 1½ cups cider vinegar
> 3 drops green food coloring (optional)
> 1 6-ounce twin pack Certo gel
> 8 6-ounce sterilized jelly jars and lids

1. Put the peppers in a heavy saucepan. Stir in the sugar and cider vinegar. Bring the mixture to a boil over medium heat. Continue boiling for 1 minute. Blend in the food coloring, if desired, and add the Certo.

2. Ladle the jelly into the sterilized jelly jars. Cool, stirring three or four times during the cooling period to keep the peppers evenly distributed.

3. Seal the jars according to the directions on the Certo package and your jars.

Makes 8 6-Ounce Jars

Pork Chops Grilled on Orange Slices

Grilling the pork chops on orange slices adds moisture and flavor to the meat. Serve with grilled asparagus, orange wedges, and Ember-Cooked Potatoes (see Index).

CITRUS MARINADE
¾ cup freshly squeezed orange juice
3 tablespoons canola oil
2 tablespoons grated orange zest
¼ cup minced cilantro
¼ teaspoon dried sage
¼ teaspoon freshly grated nutmeg

PORK
4 ¾-inch-thick pork chops, about 1 to 1½ pounds total, trimmed of all fat
1 large orange, sliced thin
¼ cup fresh sage leaves, soaked in cold water for 10 minutes and drained

1. *Prepare the Marinade:* Combine marinade ingredients and pour into a large plastic bag. Add pork chops and seal bag shut with a twist seal. Turn the bag so that all surfaces of the pork chops are coated with the marinade. Marinate, refrigerated, for 3 hours, turning the bag twice.

2. *Grill the Pork:* Prepare the grill for the direct method. Reserve the four largest orange slices and squeeze juice from remaining orange pieces onto hot coals. When the coals are ashen, sprinkle the drained sage over them. Place the four orange slices on the oiled grate and set a drained chop on each slice. Sear by grilling for 1 minute on each side. Continue grilling for 3 to 6 minutes, until the chops are tender and done to taste. Place the chops on plates and serve hot.

Makes 4 Servings

Pork Kabobs with Five-Spice Marinade

The marinade for these pork kabobs uses five-spice powder, a dark-colored blend of star anise, pepper, fennel, cloves, and cinnamon. It's available at Oriental markets and some supermarkets. These kabobs are good with extra grilled pepper strips.

FIVE-SPICE MARINADE
¼ cup canola oil
½ cup dry white wine
3 tablespoons light soy sauce or low-sodium soy sauce
3 cloves garlic, minced
½ teaspoon freshly grated gingerroot
½ teaspoon five-spice powder
½ teaspoon dry mustard

KABOBS
1 pound boneless lean pork loin, cut into 1½-inch cubes
1 large red bell pepper, seeded and cut into ½- to ¾-inch strips
12 water chestnuts, drained
4 10-inch wooden skewers, soaked in cold water for 30 minutes and drained
1 small head Boston lettuce, shredded

1. *Prepare the Marinade:* Combine the marinade ingredients in a large plastic bag. Add the pork cubes and seal the bag shut with a twist seal. Place the bag in a flat tray and turn it several times so all surfaces touch the marinade. Let the bag stand at room temperature for 2 hours, turning it twice.

2. *Grill the Kabobs:* Prepare the grill for the direct method. While the coals are heating, thread the pork cubes onto the skewers, alternating with pepper strips and water chestnuts. When the coals are ashen, place an oiled grill screen over the grate, set the kabobs on the screen, and grill for about 8 to 10 minutes, turning every 3 minutes, until the pork is tender and just pink in the center. While the kabobs are grilling, divide the shredded lettuce among four plates.

3. Remove the pork and vegetables from the skewers and arrange them on the lettuce beds. Serve immediately.

Makes 4 Servings

Iowa Double-Cut Pork Chops with Thick Apple-Raspberry Sauce

It was the Spanish conquistadors who introduced the pig, along with cattle and sheep, to North America. These thick chops are good with corn grilled in the husks.

HONEY-MUSTARD MARINADE AND BRUSHING SAUCE
¼ cup bourbon or other liquor
¼ cup prepared coarse mustard
¼ cup honey
1 cup freshly squeezed orange juice
¼ teaspoon freshly ground black pepper

PORK
4 1- to 1½-inch-thick pork chops, about 1½ pounds total
3 to 4 cups apple twigs, soaked in cold water for 30 minutes and drained (optional)
Thick Apple-Raspberry Sauce (recipe follows)

1. *Prepare the Marinade:* Combine the marinade ingredients and pour into a large plastic bag. Add the pork chops, secure shut with a twist seal, and turn the bag several times to coat all surfaces of the pork. Place the bag in a bowl and marinate, refrigerated, for 4 to 6 hours, turning the bag once.

2. *Grill the Pork:* Prepare the grill for the direct method. When the coals are ashen, add the drained twigs to them and drain the chops, reserving the marinade. Arrange the pork chops on the oiled grate and sear by grilling for 2 minutes on each side, brushing with the remaining marinade when you turn the chops. Continue grilling, covered, for 6 to 7 minutes on each side or until done to your taste. (I prefer them cooked until most traces of pinkness are gone yet not overcooked.) Serve the chops hot with Thick Apple-Raspberry Sauce.

Makes 4 Servings

Thick Apple-Raspberry Sauce

3 pounds Granny Smith apples, peeled, cored, and chopped
1 cup apple juice
¼ cup sugar
1 teaspoon ground cinnamon
1 teaspoon grated lemon zest
¼ teaspoon freshly grated nutmeg
2 cups fresh raspberries, washed

1. Mix all the ingredients in a large saucepan. Bring the mixture to a boil, then reduce the heat to low and simmer until most of the liquid has evaporated and the apples are very soft, stirring often.

2. Cool the mixture and puree it in a food processor fitted with the steel blade or in a blender. Taste it for sweetness and add 1 tablespoon sugar if desired. Ladle the sauce into a bowl and serve warm or cold. Place any leftover sauce in a covered container and refrigerate for future use.

Makes About 1 Quart

Apple-Glazed Pork Loin with Green Peppercorns

Green peppercorns add a pungent taste to pork. For a great side dish, try Grilled Belgian Endive (see box). The grilled pork is also good with sweet potatoes.

GREEN PEPPERCORN MARINADE
1 cup apple juice
½ teaspoon Worcestershire sauce
2 tablespoons apple jelly, melted
3 tablespoons freshly squeezed lime juice
½ teaspoon garlic powder
1 tablespoon crushed green peppercorns (see Index)

PORK
1 boneless pork loin, about 2 pounds, trimmed of all fat

APPLE-GREEN PEPPERCORN GLAZE
3 ounces apple jelly (you can use low-calorie jelly)
½ teaspoon Worcestershire sauce
½ teaspoon dry mustard
1 tablespoon crushed green peppercorns

1. *Prepare the Marinade:* Combine the marinade ingredients and pour into a large plastic bag. Add the pork and secure shut with a twist seal. Turn the bag several times to make sure all surfaces of the pork touch the marinade. Marinate, refrigerated, for 4 to 6 hours, turning once or twice.

2. *Prepare the Glaze:* Heat the jelly with 3 tablespoons water in a small saucepan over medium heat, stirring constantly until the jelly is melted, about 5 minutes. Blend in the Worcestershire sauce and dry mustard.

3. *Grill the Pork:*   Prepare the grill for the direct method. When the coals are ashen, drain and pat the pork loin dry with paper towels. Brush the glaze over the loin, then press the crushed green peppercorns into the meat on all sides. Place the pork on the oiled grate and sear by grilling for 2 minutes on each side. Continue grilling, covered, for about 30 to 40 minutes or until done to your taste, rotating every 10 minutes. The pork is cooked when a meat thermometer reaches 160°F or when most traces of pink are gone yet the meat is not overcooked.

4. Transfer the pork loin to a serving platter and let it stand for 5 minutes. Slice and serve.

Makes 6 to 8 Servings

GRILLED BELGIAN ENDIVE

Cut endive in half lengthwise, oil it lightly, and place on the oiled grate, cut side down, over ashen coals. Grill for about 5 minutes.

Virginia-Style Barbecue

Barbecued pork is popular in Virginia and is used as both an appetizer and an entree. As an entree it's good with Grilled Corn Pieces (recipe follows) and grilled scallions. Serve a green salad.

Citrus Marinade (see Index)
1¾ pounds boneless lean pork loin, trimmed of all fat

BARBECUE SAUCE
6 scallions, chopped
2 cloves garlic, minced
2 tablespoons canola oil
¼ cup cider vinegar
¾ cup catsup
1 cup tomato juice
½ teaspoon Worcestershire sauce
¼ cup dark brown sugar
1 teaspoon regular chili powder
½ teaspoon ground cumin
½ teaspoon salt
¼ teaspoon red pepper flakes

1 apple, sliced
3 to 4 cups apple twigs, soaked in cold water for 30 minutes and drained
2 tablespoons chili powder
6 to 8 seeded hamburger buns

1. *Marinate the Pork:* Pour the marinade into a large plastic bag. Add the pork and secure with a twist seal. Turn the bag several times so that all surfaces of the meat touch the marinade. Marinate, refrigerated, for 4 to 6 hours, turning the bag occasionally.

2. *Prepare the Sauce:* Sauté the scallions and garlic in the oil over medium heat for 4 minutes. Blend all sauce ingredients together in a medium saucepan. Bring the sauce to a boil over medium heat, reduce the heat, and simmer for 5 minutes, stirring often. Set aside.

3. *Grill the Pork:* Prepare the grill for the indirect method. Put the apple slices in water in a drip pan. When the coals are ashen, sprinkle them with the apple twigs. Drain the loin and rub it with chili powder. Place the pork on the oiled grate and sear by grilling for 2 minutes on each side. Continue grilling, covered, for 40 to 60 minutes, rotating the meat every 5 to 10 minutes.

4. Transfer the pork to a cutting board and let it stand for 5 minutes. Meanwhile, reheat the sauce. Slice or shred the meat paper-thin. Stir bits of meat into the hot barbecue sauce. Spoon it onto the buns and serve.

Makes 6 to 8 Servings

Grilled Corn Pieces

6 to 8 large ears corn, shucked
¼ teaspoon freshly ground black pepper or cayenne pepper
¼ teaspoon salt
¼ cup melted reduced-calorie margarine

1. Cut each ear into three or four pieces. Add the pepper and salt to the margarine and brush the corn with the margarine.

2. When you remove the pork from the grill, place the corn on the oiled grate or an oiled grill screen. Grill for 3 to 4 minutes, rotating after 2 minutes.

3. Transfer the corn to a platter and serve hot.

Makes 6 to 8 Servings

GRILLED SCALLIONS

Trim tops and bottoms of scallions and brush with garlic-flavored olive oil. Arrange scallions on a greased Griffo-Grill and grill until scallions are just browning.

Pork Satay with Peanut Sauce

Satay can be grilled on a hibachi as guests watch—or let them grill their own. From Indonesian cuisine, satay is popular in all of Malaysia as well as in the United States. Serve this with rice.

THAI MARINADE
¼ cup canola oil
½ teaspoon ground ginger
½ teaspoon ground cumin
2 teaspoons ground coriander
1 medium onion, minced
⅛ teaspoon freshly ground pepper
2 tablespoons freshly squeezed lemon juice or sherry
3 tablespoons light brown sugar
2 tablespoons soy sauce or light soy sauce

PORK
1¼ pounds boneless lean pork loin, trimmed of all fat and cut into 12 ½-inch-thick strips (cut along length of loin)
12 8- to 10-inch wooden skewers, soaked in cold water for 30 minutes and drained
⅓ cup chopped cilantro for garnish
1 lime, sliced, for garnish

HOT PEANUT SAUCE
1½ cups chicken stock
3 cloves garlic, minced
1 small onion, minced
¾ cup good-quality chunky peanut butter
3 tablespoons light brown sugar
½ teaspoon (or to taste) red pepper flakes
1 tablespoon minced cilantro

1. *Prepare the Marinade:* Combine the marinade ingredients and pour into a large plastic bag. Add the pork slices and secure the bag shut with a twist seal. Turn the bag several times so that all surfaces are coated with the marinade. Place the bag in a shallow dish and marinate, refrigerated, 2 to 4 hours, turning the bag once.

2. *Prepare the Sauce:* While the pork strips are marinating, heat the stock in a medium saucepan and add the garlic, onion, and peanut butter. Mix in the sugar, red pepper, and cilantro. Simmer for 3 minutes and adjust the seasonings.

3. *Grill the Pork:* Satay is best cooked over hot coals for a very short time. Use a hibachi or a regular grill. Prepare the grill for the direct method. Drain the pork and thread the strips tightly onto the skewers. When the coals are ashen, set the skewers perpendicular to the oiled grate or use an oiled grill screen. Grill for 1½ to 2 minutes on each side or until the pork is cooked through. It will cook quickly. Meanwhile, reheat the peanut sauce.

4. Serve hot, sprinkled with cilantro, garnished with lime slices, and pass the hot peanut sauce separately.

Makes 6 Servings

Hoisin-Brushed Pork Tenderloin with Scallion Curls

Hoisin sauce, available at large supermarkets and Oriental food markets, is a dark sauce made from soy beans, garlic, spices, and chili. Often served with pork dishes in Chinese restaurants, the taste is both sweet and tangy. My younger daughter, Dorothy, prefers hoisin sauce to any other prepared sauce. Be creative and try it on other meats. Serve this tenderloin with brown rice.

HOISIN MARINADE AND BRUSHING SAUCE
3 cloves garlic, minced
¼ teaspoon grated fresh gingerroot
⅓ cup honey at room temperature
3 tablespoons dry red wine
2 tablespoons soy sauce
½ cup hoisin sauce
2 tablespoons Oriental chili sauce

PORK
1 pork tenderloin, about 1 pound, trimmed of all fat
8 scallions

1. *Prepare the Marinade/Brushing Sauce:* Mix the garlic and ginger in a small bowl. Blend in the honey, wine, soy sauce, hoisin sauce, and chili sauce.

2. Pat the pork tenderloin dry with paper towels. Brush it with the marinade, set it in a shallow glass dish, and cover it with the remaining marinade. Marinate the pork at room temperature for 2 hours, turning it frequently.

3. *Prepare the Scallion Curls:* While the pork is marinating, wash the scallions and trim them at the point where they are beginning to turn green; you should have white parts about 3 inches long. Reserve the greens for another use. With a sharp, pointed knife make six ½-inch lengthwise cuts in both ends of the scallions. Put eight to ten ice cubes and the scallions in a mixing bowl and top with ice-cold water. Refrigerate for 2 hours.

4. *Grill the Pork:* Prepare the grill for the indirect method. When the coals are ashen, drain the pork, reserving the marinade. Place the loin on the oiled grate and sear by grilling for 2 minutes on each side. Continue grilling, covered, for 15 minutes or until the pork is done to your taste and no traces of pink remain, rotating the pork and brushing it with the marinade every 5 minutes.

5. Transfer the pork to a serving tray and let it stand for 5 minutes. Meanwhile, drain the scallions on paper towels. Slice the pork, garnish it with scallion curls, and serve hot.

Makes 4 Servings

Pork Tenderloin with Spiced Fig Relish

Serving this pork tenderloin with Sweet and Sour Red Cabbage (recipe follows) and an innovative Spiced Fig Relish will bring raves at your next dinner party.

WHITE WINE MARINADE
1 cup dry white wine
¼ cup extra-virgin olive oil
¼ cup light brown sugar
¼ cup chopped fresh parsley
2 bay leaves

PORK
1 1¾- to 2-pound pork tenderloin, trimmed of all fat

SPICED FIG RELISH
1 cup chopped dried figs
1 cup golden raisins
1 cup dry white wine
¼ teaspoon ground cinnamon
¼ teaspoon ground allspice
⅛ teaspoon salt
⅛ teaspoon freshly ground pepper
¼ cup light brown sugar

1. *Prepare the Marinade:* Combine the marinade ingredients and pour into a large plastic bag. Add the pork and secure the bag shut with a twist seal. Turn the bag several times so that all surfaces of the pork touch the marinade. Place the bag in a shallow dish and marinate, refrigerated, for 4 to 6 hours, turning occasionally.
2. *Prepare the Relish:* While the pork is marinating, soak the chopped figs and raisins in the wine for 30 minutes. Using a food processor fitted with the steel blade, process the figs, raisins, wine, cinnamon, allspice, salt, pepper, and sugar until finely chopped. Set aside.
3. *Grill the Pork:* Prepare the grill for the indirect method. When the coals are ashen, drain the pork and place it on the oiled grate. Sear it by grilling for 2 minutes on each side. Continue grilling, covered, for 8 minutes. Rotate the pork

and grill, covered, for 40 to 60 minutes total time or until the pork is no longer pink in the center or it is cooked to your taste. (Pork should register 160°F on a meat thermometer.)

4. Remove the tenderloin from the grill and let it stand for 5 minutes. Slice and serve over Sweet and Sour Red Cabbage with the fig relish on the side.

Makes 6 Servings

Sweet and Sour Red Cabbage

Granny Smith apples are tart, green-skinned, and smooth-fleshed. They are highly recommended for use in cooking. Prepare the cabbage while the pork in the preceding recipe is marinating.

- ¼ cup reduced-calorie margarine
- 3 large, firm apples, peeled, cored, and sliced thin
- ½ teaspoon ground cinnamon
- 1 medium head red cabbage, shredded
- ¼ teaspoon salt
- 1½ teaspoons caraway seeds
- 2 cups water
- 3 tablespoons cider vinegar
- ¼ cup light brown sugar
- ⅓ cup dry red wine

1. Melt the margarine in a medium saucepan over medium heat. Add the apples and cinnamon and sauté until tender, about 3 to 5 minutes.

2. Add the cabbage and sprinkle it with the salt, caraway seeds, water, vinegar, sugar, and wine. Reduce the heat and simmer, covered, for 30 minutes or until the cabbage is tender. Add more water if necessary.

3. To serve, arrange the cabbage on a platter with the sliced pork on top.

Makes 6 Servings

Pork Ribbon Kabobs with Cider Sauce

Apples and cider blend naturally with pork. With these kabobs, serve cider as a beverage and grill extra apple slices (see box).

CIDER SAUCE
1 tablespoon reduced-calorie margarine
1 tablespoon canola oil
3 shallots, minced
1 large apple, peeled, cored, and cubed
1½ cups fresh apple cider
1 teaspoon catsup or tomato paste
½ cup buttermilk
¼ teaspoon salt
⅛ teaspoon freshly ground white pepper
⅛ teaspoon freshly grated nutmeg

KABOBS
4 10-inch wooden skewers, soaked in cold water for 30 minutes and drained
4 pork cutlets, about 1¼ pounds total, cut along the length into 3 horizontal strips each
4 apples, cored and quartered
2 tablespoons reduced-calorie margarine
8 mild peppers, such as Anaheim, washed

1. *Prepare the Sauce:* Melt the margarine and oil in a saucepan. Add the shallots and apple and sauté over medium heat, stirring often, for about 5 minutes. Stir in the cider and catsup. Continue cooking until the liquid is reduced by one-third, about 5 minutes. Blend in the buttermilk. Season with salt, pepper, and nutmeg.

2. *Grill the Kabobs:* Prepare the grill for the indirect method. While the coals are heating, thread the pork strips onto the skewers, like ribbon candy, alternately with the apple quarters brushed with margarine. Thread the whole peppers on the ends of the skewers. Each skewer should have three strips of pork, two apple quarters, and 2 peppers. When the coals are ashen, place the skewers

on the oiled grate, perpendicular to the grate, or use an oiled grill screen. Grill for 3 to 4 minutes on each side or until done to your taste. Meanwhile, reheat the sauce.

3. Remove the skewers from the grill and arrange them on a serving platter. Serve hot, drizzled with cider sauce.

Makes 4 Servings

GRILLED APPLES

Cut apples—Granny Smiths are a good choice—into slices and brush both sides of each slice with melted reduced-calorie margarine. Place on the oiled grate and grill for 1 to 2 minutes on each side. Best served hot or warm.

A CUBAN GRILL DINNER

Black Bean Soup
Avocado Salad
Marinated Pork Loin
Grilled Bananas

"The barbacoa is a fixture in Cuban homes," says Bob Parraga, a native of Cuba and an American resident for 20 years. (Parraga together with David Kovslund own the Le Cochonett restaurant in Chicago.) "Barbacoa or barbecue gets constant use during hot summer months. The Cubans love to barbecue pork loin or shoulder. Mojito, a mixture of sour orange juice, onions, garlic, and herbs, is the national marinade of Cuba," jokes Paraga. "Cuban beef, such as steak, is grilled very simply. Just rub the meat with salt, pepper, and fresh garlic. Then, right before serving, sprinkle the meat with a little fresh lime juice. The lime juice adds the right amount of pungency to the garlicky grilled meat."

This dinner is excellent for entertaining since most of it is prepared ahead. Bean soup will be richer and thicker if prepared one day ahead and refrigerated.

Black Bean Soup

This soup can be pureed in a blender. The traditional soup is served plain or over rice, but it may be garnished with chopped onions. Sherry may be added by individual diners as a flavor enhancer.

1 pound dry black beans
1 tablespoon salt
1 bay leaf
1 medium green bell pepper, seeded and chopped
1 medium onion, chopped
1 large tomato, chopped
2 cloves garlic, crushed
3 ounces extra-virgin olive oil

¼ teaspoon freshly ground black pepper
1 teaspoon crushed dried oregano
¼ teaspoon ground cumin
¼ teaspoon cayenne pepper
2 tablespoons red wine vinegar
1 teaspoon sugar
⅓ cup dry sherry

1. Rinse the beans several times, then place them in a deep pot and add enough cold water to cover them. Soak the beans for at least 6 hours or overnight.

2. Do not discard the soaking water; add enough water to cover the beans by 1 inch. Bring the beans to a boil and reduce the heat until the liquid is simmering. Skim any foam from the top and add the salt, bay leaf, half the green pepper, half the onion, the tomato, one crushed garlic clove, 1 tablespoon of the olive oil, and the black pepper. Simmer, stirring occasionally, for about 1 hour, until the beans are tender but still firm.

3. Heat the remaining olive oil in a frying pan, add the remaining garlic and onion, and sauté over medium heat until the onions are translucent, about 4 minutes, stirring often. Add the oregano and cumin and cook for 5 minutes over low heat. Add this mixture to the beans.

4. Add the cayenne pepper, vinegar, sugar, and sherry. Simmer for 30 minutes or until the beans are soft to the point of breaking. Remove one slotted spoonful of beans and mash. Return the mashed beans to the pot and stir to thicken. Check the seasoning, discard the bay leaf, and serve.

Makes 8 to 10 Servings

Avocado Salad

Avocados will darken once peeled if exposed to air for any length of time. To prevent discoloration, sprinkle the avocado with lemon juice and cover with plastic wrap.

4 ripe medium avocados
1 head romaine lettuce
2 tablespoons extra-virgin olive oil
Wine vinegar, salt, and freshly ground pepper to taste

1. Cut the avocados in half lengthwise. Remove and discard the seed and skin.

2. Slice the lettuce and arrange on eight salad plates. Slice the avocado and arrange on the lettuce.

3. Sprinkle the salads with the olive oil, wine vinegar, salt, and pepper.

Makes 8 Servings

Marinated Pork Loin

Sour orange juice is available at times at Spanish grocery stores. You can substitute ⅔ cup orange juice plus ⅓ cup lemon juice for 1 cup sour orange juice. For dessert serve Grilled Bananas.

SOUR ORANGE MARINADE
4 medium cloves garlic, crushed
½ teaspoon crushed dried oregano
¼ teaspoon ground cumin
1 cup sour orange juice
Salt and freshly ground pepper to taste

PORK
3 pounds lean rolled pork loin, trimmed of any fat
1 small onion, sliced
1 tablespoon extra-virgin olive oil
2 limes, sliced, for garnish

1. *Prepare the Marinade:* Mix all marinade ingredients except salt and pepper in a bowl. Salt and pepper the pork to taste. Pierce the meat with a kitchen fork several times. Pour the marinade into a large plastic bag and add the pork and onion slices. Secure the bag shut with a twist seal and turn it so that all surfaces are coated with marinade. Marinate, refrigerated, for at least 12 hours, turning occasionally.

2. *Grill the Pork:* Prepare the grill for the indirect method. When the coals are ashen, remove the pork from the marinade, reserving the marinade. Brush the pork with the olive oil and place it on the oiled grate in the center of the grill. Sear by grilling for 1 minute on all sides. Continue grilling, covered, for 1 to 1½ hours or until done (pork should register 160°F on a meat thermometer), rotating every 10 minutes. Baste with marinade frequently and turn several times for even roasting.

3. Transfer the pork to a platter and let it stand for 5 minutes before slicing. Serve it garnished with lime slices.

Makes 8 to 10 Servings

Grilled Bananas

3 tablespoons freshly squeezed lime juice
8 large ripe bananas, peeled
3 tablespoons dark brown sugar
¼ cup melted margarine

1. Sprinkle the lime juice over the peeled bananas.
2. Mix together the sugar and melted margarine. Brush the bananas with the sugar-margarine mixture.
3. Place the bananas on a Griffo-Grill (see Appendix), and cook over the coals while they are cooling. Turn the bananas after 4 minutes and continue cooking them for another 3 to 5 minutes, just as they begin to brown. Serve hot as is or over vanilla ice cream if desired.

Makes 8 Servings

GRILLED PINEAPPLE
Cut fresh, trimmed, and cored pineapple into 1-inch-thick rounds. Brush with melted butter mixed with a dash of ground ginger and grill for 2 minutes on each side.

VEAL

Veal is one of the leanest and most versatile meats you can buy. A 3-ounce portion of cooked, trimmed veal has fewer than 166 calories and about 60 percent of the protein you need for a whole day. This size portion has 100 milligrams of cholesterol, one-third the daily recommended maximum of 300 milligrams. While veal is somewhat higher in cholesterol than beef, the lower amount of total fat (unless fat is added in cooking) makes it a healthy choice. Veal is also rich in niacin, vitamin B_{12}, and zinc.

When you're buying veal, look for a creamy pink color and fine grain. Any fat covering should be milky white. Because veal is from young animals, it has less fat but also provides less iron than beef.

Lemon Veal with Pink Pasta

For cooking and some marinades we use extra-virgin olive oil for its distinctive flavor and high quality. Grilling thin slices of veal on a slice of lemon helps retain juices and adds flavor.

LEMON-SAGE MARINADE
⅓ cup freshly squeezed lemon juice
2 cloves garlic, minced
½ cup canola oil
1 tablespoon crushed dried sage
¼ cup chopped fresh parsley
⅛ teaspoon freshly ground white pepper

VEAL
1½ pounds ½-inch-thick veal cutlets
2 large lemons, sliced thin

PINK PASTA
1 cup all-purpose flour
1 cup instant flour
2 tablespoons pureed drained canned beets
½ teaspoon salt
2 eggs

2 teaspoons extra-virgin olive oil
5 quarts water
3 tablespoons salt
2 tablespoons cider vinegar
2 tablespoons canola oil

YOGURT BEET SAUCE
2 cups plain low-fat yogurt
1 cup chopped drained canned beets
2 teaspoons fresh dill

1. *Prepare the Marinade:* Combine the marinade ingredients and pour into a large plastic bag. Add the veal cutlets and seal the bag shut with a twist seal. Turn the bag several times so that all the surfaces of the veal touch the marinade. Place the bag in a shallow dish and marinate, refrigerated, for 3 to 4 hours.

2. *Prepare the Pasta:* While the veal is marinating, put the flours in a mixing bowl. Make a well in the center and add the pureed beet, salt, eggs, and olive oil to the well. Mix the dough together with your fingers until the dough can be gathered into a ball. Knead the dough on a lightly floured board until smooth and elastic, about 8 minutes. Add more flour if the dough seems sticky. Gather the dough together and wrap it in waxed paper; let the dough rest for 10 minutes before rolling it out.

3. Using a rolling pin or a pasta machine, roll the dough paper-thin. Roll up the dough from the long end, jelly-roll style. Cut the dough into ¼-inch-wide strips. Unroll each strip and spread on waxed paper or on a pasta dryer to air-dry.

4. *Cook the Pasta:* Bring the water to a rapid boil in a large pot. Add the salt, vinegar, and oil, then the pasta. Cook until just tender, al dente, 2 to 3 minutes; drain.

5. *Prepare the Sauce:* Stir the yogurt, beets, and dill together in a bowl. Refrigerate until needed. Bring to room temperature before serving.

6. *Grill the Veal:* Prepare the grill for the indirect method. When the coals are ashen, set one or two slices of lemon for each cutlet on the oiled grate or an oiled grill screen. Set the drained cutlets on top of the lemon slices and grill quickly, about 2 minutes per side or until done to your taste. Meanwhile, refresh the pasta under hot running water, drain it, transfer it to a heated platter, and toss it with the sauce. Serve the veal hot with the lemon slices and the pasta.

Makes 4 Servings

Veal Ribbon Kabobs with Chestnuts and Prunes

The nutmeg tree gives us two treats: nutmeg and mace. Mace is made by sun-drying the nutmeg seed. Its spicy yet sweet flavor makes it perfect with fruits, desserts, and, as used here, with the mild-flavored veal. Grown in the British West Indies, Indonesia, and Sri Lanka, mace is sold ground in most supermarkets.

For this recipe, use drained canned chestnuts or our recipe for Chestnuts Roasted on the Embers (see Index).

Wild rice and green beans are good accompaniments.

BRUSHING SAUCE
2 tablespoons apple jelly
½ cup apple juice
1 teaspoon grated lemon zest
¼ teaspoon ground cinnamon
¼ teaspoon ground ginger
¼ teaspoon ground mace
¼ teaspoon ground allspice

KABOBS
16 large pitted prunes
½ cup dry red wine
16 drained canned or peeled roasted chestnuts
4 10-inch wooden skewers, soaked in cold water for 30 minutes and drained
4 veal cutlets, about 5 ounces each, cut along the length of the meat into 4 horizontal strips, each about 6 inches
4 dried pears
4 dried apricots

1. *Prepare the Brushing Sauce:* Heat the apple jelly in a small pan over medium heat. Stir in the remaining sauce ingredients and simmer for 3 to 4 minutes, stirring often. Cool slightly.

2. *Prepare the Prunes:* Soak the prunes in the wine for 1 hour. Drain and stuff each prune with a chestnut.

3. *Grill the Kabobs:* Prepare the grill for the direct method. While the coals are heating, thread the skewers alternately with veal (threaded "in and out" like ribbon candy), stuffed prunes, pears, and apricots, beginning with veal and ending with an apricot. Brush with the sauce. When the coals are ashen, place the skewers on the oiled grate, perpendicular to the grate, or on an oiled grill screen. Grill for 3 to 4 minutes on each side, until the veal is cooked. Do not overcook.

4. Remove the kabobs from the grill and place them on a serving platter. Serve hot.

Makes 4 Servings

Hungarian Veal Cutlets

Cutlets are thin and require less time on the grill than other cuts. Be careful not to overcook them. Serve with spaetzle or noodles.

HUNGARIAN SAUCE
2 tablespoons canola oil
1 large onion, minced
2 cloves garlic, minced
1 teaspoon paprika
3 tablespoons catsup
3 tablespoons dry red wine
Salt and freshly ground pepper to taste

VEAL
½ teaspoon paprika
¼ cup catsup
4 ½- to ¾-inch-thick veal cutlets, about 1 to 1¼ pounds total
8 teaspoons low-fat sour cream or plain low-fat yogurt for garnish

1. *Prepare the Sauce:* Heat the oil in a frying pan over medium heat and add the onion and garlic. Sauté for 3 to 5 minutes or until soft, stirring occasionally. Stir in 1 teaspoon paprika, 3 tablespoons catsup, and the wine. Season with salt and freshly ground black pepper to taste. Remove the pan from the heat.

2. *Grill the Veal:* Prepare the grill for the indirect method. Mix ½ teaspoon paprika with ¼ cup catsup and brush the cutlets with this sauce. When the coals are ashen, place the cutlets on the oiled grate and sear by grilling them for 1 minute on each side. Continue grilling the veal in the center of the grill until cooked to your taste, about 2 minutes per side.

3. Transfer the cutlets to dinner plates and spread them with the warm sauce. Garnish each with a dollop of about 2 teaspoons sour cream or yogurt.

Makes 4 Servings

Veal Chops with Apples, Onions, and Yogurt

Who needs gravy when there are delicious, flavorful toppings like this for meat? Serve these chops with grilled onion slices and salad.

TOPPING
2 tablespoons reduced-calorie margarine
2 large onions, sliced
2 large, firm apples, such as Golden Delicious, cored and sliced
½ teaspoon crumbled dried thyme
¼ teaspoon salt
¼ teaspoon ground cinnamon
⅛ teaspoon freshly ground pepper

VEAL
1 tablespoon crumbled dried thyme
¼ teaspoon freshly ground pepper
2 tablespoons extra-virgin olive oil
4 ¾-inch-thick veal rib chops, about 1¼ pounds total
¼ cup crumbled dried thyme, soaked in water for 10 minutes and drained
¼ cup plain low-fat yogurt for garnish

1. *Prepare the Topping:* Heat the margarine in a large, heavy frying pan over medium heat, add the onions and sauté until soft, about 5 minutes, stirring occasionally. Add the apple slices and continue cooking until the apples are tender, about 4 minutes. Season with thyme, salt, cinnamon, and pepper. Set aside.

2. *Grill the Veal:* Prepare the grill for the direct method. When the coals are ashen, combine the thyme, pepper, and olive oil in a small bowl and brush this over the veal chops. Sprinkle the coals with the drained thyme and place the veal chops on the oiled grate. Sear by grilling for 1 minute on each side. Continue grilling the chops for 4 to 6 minutes, turning once or twice. Best cooked medium or medium-rare.

3. Place a veal chop on each dinner plate with warm apples and onions. Top each chop with a dollop of low-fat yogurt. Serve immediately.

Makes 4 Servings

Mixed Grill with English Mustard Dipping Sauce

The "mixed grill" originated in the British Isles. This recipe, which features beef and veal, goes well with the tangy sauce made with hot English mustard. Serve with Ember-Cooked Potatoes (see Index) and Sweet Onion Preserves (recipe follows). Ale is the perfect beverage.

ENGLISH MUSTARD DIPPING SAUCE
¼ cup prepared English mustard
2 cups dark beer
¼ cup dark brown sugar
2 tablespoons chopped watercress
1 teaspoon crumbled dried rosemary

MEATS
1 cup fresh rosemary sprigs, soaked in cold water for 10 minutes and drained
1 pound skirt steak
6 ¾-inch-thick veal loin chops, about 3 to 4 ounces each
3 large tomatoes, cut in half
3 Golden Delicious apples, cut in half

1. *Prepare the Sauce:* Combine the sauce ingredients, cover, and refrigerate until needed.

2. *Grill the Meats:* Prepare the grill for the direct method. When the coals are ashen, sprinkle them with the rosemary. Replace the oiled grate or use an oiled grill screen. Brush the meats and tomatoes lightly with the dipping sauce. Place the steaks on the grill first, then the chops, and finally the tomatoes and apples. This way they will finish cooking together. Grill the steaks for 8 to 10 minutes, turning them once. Grill the chops for 6 to 7 minutes. The tomatoes and apples will take about 4 minutes. Place the tomatoes and apples on the grate cut side down for the first minute, then turn them.

3. Cut the steaks into six equal portions and arrange the steaks and chops in the center of a platter. Arrange the tomatoes and apples around the meat.

Makes 6 Servings

Sweet Onion Preserves

¼ cup reduced-calorie margarine
3 cups thinly sliced white onion
⅓ cup sugar
¼ cup white wine vinegar
⅛ teaspoon freshly ground white pepper
¾ cup chopped dried apricot
¾ cup dry white wine

1. Melt the margarine in a medium saucepan over medium heat. Add the onions and lightly sauté them for 5 minutes, stirring often.
2. Mix in the remaining ingredients and stir to combine.
3. Reduce the heat and simmer, stirring often, for 15 to 20 minutes. Let the preserves cool. The mixture will be thick.
4. Spoon the preserves into a serving dish and cover lightly. Refrigerate until ready to serve. Best served at room temperature.

Makes 2½ Cups

Loin Veal Chops with Garlic and Mushrooms

You may want to combine porcini mushrooms with the shiitake mushrooms if porcini mushrooms are available. Shiitakes have a full-bodied and meaty taste. They were originally cultivated in the East and are available either dried or fresh, but this recipe uses the fresh ones. Serve with grilled or steamed asparagus.

> Lemon-Sage Marinade (see Index)
> 4 ¾-inch-thick veal loin chops, about 1½ pounds total
> 8 cloves elephant garlic
> ½ pound fresh shiitake mushrooms, trimmed

1. *Marinate the Veal:* Pour the marinade into a large plastic bag and add the chops. Seal the bag securely with a twist seal and turn it several times so that all sides of chops touch the marinade. Place the bag in a shallow dish and marinate, refrigerated, for 4 hours, turning the bag occasionally.

2. *Grill the Veal:* Prepare the grill for the indirect method. When the coals are ashen, drain the chops, reserving the marinade, and place them on the oiled grate. Sear the chops by grilling for 1 minute on each side. Continue grilling for about 9 minutes, turning once or twice. Place the garlic cloves at the edge of the grill at the same time. Grill the mushrooms, brushing them lightly with the marinade or vegetable oil, for about 2 minutes on each side.

3. To serve, place one chop, two cloves of garlic, and a few mushrooms on each plate. Serve hot.

Makes 4 Servings

Veal Chops with Red Wine Vinegar Sauce

Bay leaves, or laurel, date back to the early Olympic games, where they were used in garlands for winners. Native to the Mediterranean area and to Turkey, this spicy and pungent leaf accents many soups and sauces. Be sure to remove and discard the bay leaves before serving. These chops go well with grilled red bell pepper strips.

RED WINE VINEGAR SAUCE
1 tablespoon extra-virgin olive oil
2 cloves garlic, minced
2 large tomatoes, peeled, seeded, and chopped, *or* 1¾ cups drained, chopped canned tomatoes
1½ teaspoons catsup
Scant ¼ cup red wine vinegar
2 bay leaves
½ teaspoon salt
¼ teaspoon dried thyme
¼ teaspoon freshly ground black pepper

VEAL
2 tablespoons extra-virgin olive oil
4 ¾-inch-thick veal rib chops, about 1¼ pounds total
4 large bay leaves

1. *Prepare the Sauce:* Heat the olive oil in a saucepan over medium heat. Add the garlic and sauté for 1 minute, until soft, stirring once. Stir in the remaining sauce ingredients. Raise the heat to high, bring the sauce to a boil, and reduce the heat to medium. Continue cooking for 3 to 4 minutes, stirring occasionally. Set aside.
2. *Grill the Veal:* Prepare the grill for the indirect method. When the coals are ashen, brush the olive oil over the veal chops and place a bay leaf on each chop, patting it so it adheres to the meat. Place the veal chops on the oiled grate and sear by grilling for 1 minute on each side. Continue grilling for 4 to 6 minutes on each side. Best cooked medium or medium-rare. Reheat the sauce if necessary.
3. Place the chops on individual dinner plates and drizzle with the sauce.

Makes 4 Servings

Veal Chop with Mango Coulis

An exotic blend of flavors to complement grilled veal chops. Try brown rice and grilled pineapple as accompaniments.

MANGO COULIS
6 medium mangoes, peeled and cut into small pieces
2 tablespoons chopped fresh basil leaves
½ teaspoon chopped fresh mint leaves
2 teaspoons balsamic vinegar
¼ teaspoon salt
¼ teaspoon freshly ground pepper
¼ teaspoon dried thyme

VEAL
Lemon-Sage Marinade (see Index)
4 ¾-inch-thick veal rib chops, about 1¼ pounds total

1. *Prepare the Coulis:* Puree the coulis ingredients in a food processor fitted with the steel blade. Transfer the puree to a saucepan and simmer for about 3 minutes, stirring often. Refrigerate until needed.

2. *Marinate the Veal:* Pour the marinade into a large plastic bag and add the veal. Secure the bag shut with a twist seal and turn it several times so that all surfaces of the meat touch the marinade. Place the bag in a shallow dish and marinate, refrigerated, for 3 to 4 hours, turning occasionally.

3. *Grill the Veal:* Prepare the grill for the direct method. When the coals are ashen, drain the chops and place them on the oiled grate. Sear the veal by grilling it for 1 minute on each side. Continue grilling for 4 to 6 minutes on each side or until done to your taste. Meanwhile, reheat the sauce if you want to serve it warm; otherwise, serve it cold.

4. Transfer the chops to individual plates and spoon mango coulis onto the plates to one side of the chops. Serve warm.

Makes 4 Servings

Easy Veal Loin Chops with Blackberries

Fruit adds flavor and moisture to lean veal.

- 6 ½- to ¾-inch-thick veal loin chops, about 2 pounds total
- 2 tablespoons extra-virgin olive oil
- 1 teaspoon garlic powder
- 3 cups fresh blackberries or other berries of your choice
- 2 tablespoons chopped fresh mint
- 3 tablespoons blackberry brandy

1. Brush the chops with the oil and sprinkle them with the garlic powder.
2. Crush 1 cup of the berries. Combine all the berries in a bowl and stir in the mint and brandy. Set aside.
3. Prepare the grill for the indirect method. When the coals are ashen, place the chops on the oiled grate. Sear by grilling for 1 minute on each side. Continue grilling for about 9 minutes, turning the chops once or twice.
4. Transfer the chops to individual plates and spoon the sauce over them. Serve hot.

Makes 6 Servings

GRILLED ASPARAGUS

Trim the tough bottoms from a pound of fresh asparagus (if spears are especially thick, cut them in half lengthwise). Brush spears with melted butter or margarine mixed with a dash of oregano and arrange them (cut side down) on a greased Griffo-Grill over ashen coals. Grill for 10 minutes, turning occasionally. Asparagus will be just browning.

If you prefer, wrap the buttered asparagus in foil and place at the outer edge of the grill. Again, cook for 10 minutes, turning occasionally.

Veal and Pork Kabobs with Fruit

Try grilling some of the soft fruits of summer, such as papaya, honeydew, and cantaloupe (see box).

WHOLE-GRAIN MUSTARD MARINADE
¼ cup canola oil
¼ cup whole-grain English mustard
⅓ cup white wine vinegar
1 cup dry white wine
1 teaspoon grated lemon zest
1 clove garlic, mashed
½ teaspoon ground ginger

KABOBS
1 pound boneless leg of pork, cut into 1½-inch cubes
1 pound boneless leg of veal, cut into 1½-inch pieces
2 cups cubed cantaloupe (1-inch pieces)
8 scallions, cut into 1½-inch slices
2 cups cubed honeydew (1-inch pieces)
8 10- to 12-inch wooden skewers, soaked in cold water for 30 minutes and drained
3 cups peach, plum, or apple twigs, soaked in cold water for 30 minutes and drained

1. *Prepare the Marinade:* Combine the marinade ingredients and pour into a large plastic bag. Add the pork and veal and secure shut with a twist seal. Turn the bag several times to make sure all the meat surfaces touch the marinade. Place the bag in a bowl and marinate, refrigerated, 4 to 6 hours, turning occasionally.

2. *Grill the Kabobs:* Prepare the charcoal for the direct method. While the coals are heating, thread the kabobs. Drain the meats, reserving the marinade. Alternately thread on the skewers veal, cantaloupe, pork, scallion, and honeydew until all skewers are threaded evenly and all ingredients are used. When the coals are ashen, sprinkle the twigs on them and set the kabobs on the oiled grate,

perpendicular to the grate, or on an oiled grill screen. Grill the kabobs, rotating them every 2 to 3 minutes and brushing them with the reserved marinade, until the meat is cooked to your taste. Do not overcook the meat as it tends to get tough.

3. Arrange the kabobs decoratively over rice or noodles if desired, allowing guests to slide the meat and fruit from the skewers. Serve with extra grilled fruit slices.

Makes 8 Servings

GRILLED SUMMER FRUITS

Slice papaya, cantaloupe, or honeydew melon and brush the slices lightly with honey or reduced-calorie margarine (or leave the slices plain). Place them on an oiled grill screen and grill over ashen coals for 1 minute on each side.

Cold Grilled Veal with Tuna Sauce

Try this classic Italian veal dish, with its unique sauce, for an easy summer buffet. Prepare it ahead of time and serve it either cold or at room temperature, with roasted or grilled bell peppers and a large salad.

TUNA SAUCE
1 3-ounce can Italian imported tuna
1 egg yolk
3 flat anchovies, drained, patted dry, and cut in half
1½ tablespoons freshly squeezed lemon juice
⅓ cup half-and-half
3 tablespoons chicken or veal stock
⅛ teaspoon salt
⅛ teaspoon freshly ground pepper
⅛ teaspoon garlic powder
2 tablespoons minced fresh parsley
½ cup extra-virgin olive oil

VEAL
2 to 4 handfuls of fresh basil, soaked in cold water for 10 minutes and drained (optional)
2 tablespoons extra-virgin olive oil
1 2-pound veal loin *or* 6 ¾-inch-thick veal loin chops (about 2 pounds total)
½ teaspoon garlic powder

1. *Prepare the Sauce:* Using a food processor fitted with the steel blade, puree the tuna, egg yolk, and anchovies. Add the lemon juice, half-and-half, stock, salt, pepper, garlic powder, and parsley and mix well. With the machine running, pour the oil through the feed tube until it is incorporated. Place the sauce in a bowl, cover, and refrigerate until needed.

2. *Grill the Veal:* Prepare the grill for the indirect method. When the coals are ashen, sprinkle them with the basil. Rub the loin with the oil and sprinkle it with garlic powder. Place it on the oiled grate and sear by grilling 1 minute on each side. Continue grilling, covered, for about 12 to 15 minutes, rotating it every 4 to 5 minutes. Test for doneness with a meat thermometer.

3. Transfer the veal to a platter and let it cool to room temperature or chill it. Slice it paper-thin. Stir the tuna sauce, adjust the seasonings, and drizzle it over the veal.

Makes 6 to 8 Servings

GRILLED BELL PEPPERS

Cut whole peppers into ½-inch circles, discarding seeds. Brush with Italian salad dressing and place on a greased Griffo-Grill over hot coals. Grill for 2 minutes on each side.

LAMB

The juicy tenderness and delicate flavor of today's lamb make it a favorite selection for a wide variety of occasions ranging from special gourmet feasts to economical family suppers.

When you're selecting lamb, look for meat that is pinkish-red and has a velvety texture. Since lamb comes from young animals, there is little marbling and only a thin layer of fat around the outside of the meat.

Take extra care with lean lamb on the grill to prevent overcooking. Internal temperatures for lean lamb are 140°F for rare and 160°F for medium. Never cook lamb to a temperature above 160°F. If you do, the resulting dish will be less tender and flavorful.

Since there's little marbling, you have to count on the natural juices in lamb for moisture. We recommend marinating leaner cuts and searing the meat quickly on both sides before finishing the grilling.

Loin Lamb Chops with Tomato, Olive, and Garlic Kabobs

Savory rosemary complements the deep-flavored lamb. Americans tend to overcook lamb but are now starting to serve it rare. Try Marinated Garbanzo Beans (recipe follows) as a side dish.

- 6 lean lamb loin chops, about 4½ ounces each, trimmed of all fat
- 1½ teaspoons dried rosemary
- ½ teaspoon garlic powder
- 6 8-inch wooden skewers, soaked in cold water for 30 minutes and drained *or* 6 8-inch firm rosemary stems, leaves removed, a point shaped at end of stem
- 18 cloves garlic
- 2 tomatoes, cut into wedges
- 18 pitted large black olives
- ½ cup dried rosemary, soaked in water for 10 minutes and drained

1. Prepare the grill for the direct method.
2. While the coals are heating, sprinkle the chops with 1½ teaspoons rosemary and the garlic powder. Thread the skewers alternately with garlic, tomatoes, and olives.
3. When the coals are ashen, sprinkle ½ cup rosemary over them. An oiled grill screen is helpful for grilling kabobs. If one isn't available, place the kabobs perpendicular to the oiled grate. Grill the chops and kabobs at the same time. Sear the chops by grilling for 1 minute on each side. Continue grilling for 2 to 3 minutes on each side or until done to your taste. Rotate the kabobs every 2 minutes.
4. Transfer the chops and kabobs to a platter and serve hot.

Makes 6 Servings

Marinated Garbanzo Beans

3 cups drained canned garbanzo beans (chick-peas)
¼ cup freshly squeezed lemon juice
¼ cup cider vinegar
¾ cup extra-virgin olive oil
2 large cloves garlic, minced
1 bunch scallions, trimmed and chopped
1 large carrot, shredded
3 stalks celery, minced
1 2-ounce can pimiento, drained
¼ cup minced cilantro

1. Place the beans in a ceramic bowl. Mix the lemon juice, vinegar, and olive oil and toss this marinade with the beans. Mix in the garlic, scallions, carrot, celery, pimiento, and cilantro and toss all the ingredients together.
2. Cover the bowl and marinate the beans in the refrigerator overnight, stirring occasionally.
3. Drain the beans before serving. Serve cold.

Makes 6 Servings

Lamb Chops with Thyme

Our grandmothers always served mint jelly with lamb. Here we suggest ember-cooked Beets in Jackets with Dill Yogurt Sauce (see Index) and Mint Salsa (recipe follows) as accompaniments, with Mint Ice (recipe follows) served after the entree.

- ½ teaspoon dried thyme
- ½ teaspoon salt
- ¼ teaspoon freshly ground pepper
- 2 tablespoons extra-virgin olive oil
- 6 lean lamb loin chops, about 4½ ounces each, trimmed of all fat

1. Combine the thyme, salt, pepper, and olive oil and rub the mixture on both sides of the chops.
2. Prepare the grill for the direct method. When the coals are ashen, put the chops on the oiled grate and sear by grilling for 1 minute on each side. Continue grilling for 2 to 3 minutes on each side or until done to your taste. Serve hot.

Makes 6 Servings

Mint Salsa

Mint is perhaps the easiest of all herbs to cultivate. If you don't have a garden, try growing a pot of mint indoors.

- **2 large tomatoes**
- ¼ cup chopped scallion
- ¼ cup chopped fresh mint
- ¼ cup chopped fresh parsley
- ¼ teaspoon salt

1. Plunge the tomatoes into boiling water for 30 seconds or until the skins are loose. Peel the tomatoes and squeeze them gently to remove the seeds. Chop the tomatoes and put them in a bowl.
2. Toss the tomatoes with the scallions, mint, parsley, and salt. Taste and adjust the seasonings. Refrigerate until serving time. Toss again before serving.

Makes 2¾ Cups

Mint Ice

Mint Ice makes a refreshing palate freshener when served after lamb chops.

2 cups superfine sugar
3½ cups water
¾ cup freshly squeezed lemon juice
1 cup minced fresh mint leaves

1. Stir sugar and water together in a saucepan. Cook over medium heat for 6 minutes, stirring occasionally.
2. Mix in lemon juice and pour the syrup over the mint leaves in a shallow dish. Cover tightly and freeze.
3. Break up the ice and puree it in a food processor fitted with the steel blade. Freeze again.
4. Before serving, puree the ice again and spoon it into frosted glasses. Serve immediately.

Makes 6 to 8 Servings

Mediterranean Lamb Kabobs

For kabobs, lamb cubes that are cut from the leg are far superior in leanness, tenderness, and taste to meat from other parts of the lamb. Serve these over couscous and sprinkle them with raisins and almonds.

MEDITERRANEAN MARINADE
- ⅓ cup dry red wine
- ⅔ cup red wine vinegar
- ¼ cup extra-virgin olive oil
- ¼ teaspoon ground cinnamon
- ⅛ teaspoon ground allspice
- ⅛ teaspoon freshly grated nutmeg

KABOBS
- 1¼ pounds boneless lean leg of lamb, trimmed of all fat and cut into 1- to 1½-inch cubes
- 1 medium eggplant, peeled and cut into 1½-inch wedges
- 2 large tomatoes, each cut into 6 wedges
- 2 large onions, peeled and each cut into 6 wedges
- 4 large cloves garlic, unpeeled
- ½ cup crumbled feta cheese for garnish
- 6 10-inch wooden skewers, soaked in cold water for 30 minutes and drained, *or* 6 long, woody oregano stems, leaves removed, a point shaped at end of stem
- ½ cup crumbled dried oregano, soaked in cold water for 10 minutes and drained

1. *Prepare the Marinade:* Combine the marinade ingredients and pour into a large plastic bag. Add the lamb and secure the bag shut with a twist seal. Turn the bag several times so that all surfaces of the meat touch the marinade. Place the bag in a shallow dish and marinate for 2 hours at room temperature.

2. *Grill the Kabobs:* Prepare the grill for the direct method. While the coals are heating, drain the lamb, reserving the marinade, and thread the skewers with the lamb, eggplant, tomatoes, onions, and garlic cloves. Brush the kabobs with marinade. When the coals are ashen, sprinkle them with the oregano. Place the kabobs on the oiled grate, perpendicular to the grate, or on an oiled grill screen. Grill for 9 minutes, turning them every 3 minutes, or until the lamb is tender. Serve immediately.

Makes 6 Servings

Turkish Lamb Kabobs with Honeydew Wedges

Last summer my husband, Jerry, my younger daughter, Dorothy, and I traveled to Turkey. We sipped Raki, the Turkish licorice-flavored aperitif, at a beach on warm evenings. These kabobs are delicately marinated with Raki, and the flavors of Turkey can be found throughout the recipe. Serve them over hot rice with grilled tomatoes and Hearts of Palm Salad with Walnut Oil Dressing (recipe follows).

ANISE-ORANGE MARINADE
½ cup Raki or Pernod
½ cup chopped flat-leaf parsley
½ cup freshly squeezed orange juice

KABOBS
1 pound boneless lean leg of lamb, trimmed of all fat and cut into 1½-inch cubes
4 8-inch wooden skewers, soaked in cold water for 30 minutes and drained
2 medium red or green bell peppers, seeded and cut into 2-inch chunks
8 scallions, cut into 2-inch pieces
2 cups cubed honeydew (1½-inch pieces)
¼ teaspoon salt
¼ teaspoon freshly ground pepper
4 2-inch wedges of honeydew

1. *Prepare the Marinade:* Combine the marinade ingredients and pour into a large plastic bag. Add the lamb and secure the bag shut with a twist seal. Turn the bag several times so that all surfaces of the meat touch the marinade. Put the bag in a large bowl and marinate for 30 minutes at room temperature, turning once.

2. *Grill the Kabobs:* Prepare the grill for the direct method. While the coals are heating, remove the lamb from the marinade and thread the lamb cubes onto the skewers alternately with the pepper chunks, scallions, and honeydew cubes. Sprinkle the lamb, peppers, and scallions with salt and pepper. When the coals are ashen, place the skewers on the oiled grate, perpendicular to the grate, or on an oiled grill screen. Grill, uncovered, for 7 to 9 minutes turning every 3 minutes, or until the lamb is tender. Toward the end of the grilling, place the honeydew wedges on the grill and cook for 1 minute on each side.

3. Transfer the skewers and honeydew wedges to a serving platter and serve hot.

Makes 4 Servings

Hearts of Palm Salad with Walnut Oil Dressing

Hearts of palm are available canned at specialty food stores and many large supermarkets. They are the edible inside parts of the stem of the cabbage palm tree. They have a delicate, somewhat nutty flavor and are usually cut into bite-sized pieces for salads.

WALNUT OIL DRESSING
6 tablespoons walnut oil
2 tablespoons freshly squeezed lemon juice
1 clove garlic, minced
½ teaspoon superfine sugar
3 tablespoons minced fresh parsley
Salt and freshly ground black pepper to taste

SALAD
1 head romaine lettuce, washed, dried, and chilled
1 14-ounce can hearts of palm, cut into ¼-inch slices
3 scallions, minced
1 2-ounce jar pimiento, drained

1. *Prepare the Dressing:* Whisk the oil, lemon juice, and garlic together in a small bowl. Blend in the sugar and parsley and add salt and pepper to taste. Place the dressing in a covered container and refrigerate until needed.
2. *Prepare the Salad:* Tear the lettuce into bite-sized pieces. Arrange it on six chilled salad plates. Sprinkle the hearts of palm evenly over the lettuce. Add the scallions and pimiento over the hearts of palm. Shake the dressing over the salad to serve.

Makes 6 Servings

Mongolian Lamb Grill

Give your guests bowls of flavoring sauce and let them grill their own lamb on a hibachi. Serve with cooked white rice and a cucumber salad. Orange sherbet or Mint Ice (see Index) and fortune cookies are perfect for dessert. Reduced-sodium soy sauce is available at most large supermarkets, as is hoisin sauce, and Oriental chili sauce is available at Chinese food stores.

FLAVORING SAUCE
⅓ cup chopped scallion
⅓ cup minced fresh parsley
3 tablespoons reduced-sodium soy sauce
¼ teaspoon Oriental chili sauce
½ teaspoon dark sesame oil
½ teaspoon sesame seeds

DIPPING SAUCE
3 cloves garlic, minced
½ teaspoon red pepper flakes
½ cup hoisin sauce
1 tablespoon dark soy sauce
½ teaspoon sugar

LAMB AND VEGETABLES
1 cup snow peas, trimmed
8 scallions, trimmed
Peanut oil for brushing snow peas and scallions
1 pound boneless lean leg of lamb, trimmed of all fat and sliced paper-thin*
4 pairs chopsticks

1. *Prepare the Flavoring Sauce:* Combine the flavoring sauce ingredients in a bowl. Divide the sauce into four small bowls (Oriental dishes add a nice flair) and place them at each setting.

2. *Prepare the Dipping Sauce:* Combine the dipping sauce ingredients in a small bowl. Divide it into two sauce dishes and set one at each end of the table.

---

*For easy slicing, freeze lamb until it's firm but can still be pierced with the tines of a fork.

3. *Prepare the Lamb and Vegetables:* Brush the snow peas and scallions with peanut oil and place on a platter. Set the lamb slices decoratively on the platter and take the platter to the table.

4. Set the hibachi on a firm table over a trivet to protect the table. Light the charcoal. When the coals are ashen, replace the grate and set an oiled grill screen over the top.

5. Using chopsticks, have each guest dip a lamb slice in the sauce and quickly grill it. Have the guests grill scallions and snow peas at the same time.

Makes 4 Servings

Butterflied Leg of Lamb with Potato Garlic Sauce

My son-in-law just returned from his yearly visit to Salonika, Greece, to see his parents. The only gift I asked him for was one recipe from his mother. This year Leonidus suggested making grilled butterflied leg of lamb with potato garlic sauce. It's good with grilled eggplant and Greek salad.

Red Wine Marinade I (see Index)
1 4- to 5-pound leg of lamb, butterflied by butcher

SALONIKA GARLIC SAUCE
2 medium-large potatoes, peeled and boiled
4 cloves garlic, peeled
1 egg yolk
¼ cup extra-virgin olive oil
¼ cup freshly squeezed lemon juice
½ teaspoon salt
¼ teaspoon freshly ground white pepper

½ cup dried oregano, soaked in cold water for 10 minutes and drained (optional)
2 tablespoons extra-virgin olive oil
1 teaspoon dried oregano
1 lemon, cut in half

1. *Marinate the Lamb:* Place the lamb in a large, shallow ceramic dish and add the marinade. Marinate, refrigerated, for 6 to 8 hours or overnight, turning occasionally.
2. *Prepare the Sauce:* Cut the potatoes into 1-inch pieces. Using a food processor fitted with the steel blade, puree the garlic. Add the potatoes and egg yolk. With the machine running, pour the olive oil through the feed tube until the mixture is blended. Add the lemon juice, salt, and pepper. Combine the ingredients and adjust seasonings. The mixture should be thick. Cover and refrigerate until needed.

3. *Grill the Lamb:* Prepare the grill for the indirect method. For added flavor, add the oregano to the water pan. When the coals are ashen, drain the lamb and brush it with 2 tablespoons oil, sprinkle it with 1 teaspoon oregano, and squeeze the lemon over it. Set the lamb on the oiled grate, cover, and grill for 35 to 45 minutes or until done, turning the lamb every 10 to 15 minutes. Lamb is best pink in center. As with all meats, do not overcook. Because of the uneven shape of butterflied lamb, some areas will be rarer than others. Test the thickest part of the leg for doneness. While the lamb is grilling, remove the sauce from the refrigerator and bring it to room temperature.

4. Transfer the lamb to a serving platter, let it stand for 5 minutes, and slice thin. Bring the lamb to the table and serve it with the Salonika sauce in a sauceboat.

Makes 10 to 12 Servings

Butterflied Leg of Lamb with Rosemary Marinade

Rosemary has hints of both pine and citrus flavors. Originally grown in the Mediterranean countries, it is widely available both dried and fresh. Use fresh rosemary when possible. With the lamb, serve Marinated Grilled Red Pepper Strips (recipe follows) and rice pilaf.

ROSEMARY MARINADE
- ⅓ cup canola oil
- ⅔ cup freshly squeezed orange juice
- 2 tablespoons balsamic vinegar
- 2 scallions, minced
- 2 teaspoons crumbled dried rosemary
- ¼ teaspoon freshly ground pepper

LAMB
- 1 4- to 5-pound leg of lamb, butterflied by butcher
- ½ cup dried rosemary, soaked in cold water for 10 minutes and drained

1. *Prepare the Marinade:* Combine the marinade ingredients. Place the lamb in a large, shallow ceramic dish and add the marinade. Marinate, refrigerated, for 6 to 8 hours or overnight, turning once.

2. *Grill the Lamb:* Prepare the grill for the indirect method. When the coals are ashen sprinkle the coals with rosemary. Drain the lamb and place it on the oiled grate. Cover and grill for 35 to 45 minutes or until done, turning the lamb every 10 to 15 minutes. The lamb is best pink in center. As with all meats, do not overcook. Some areas will be rarer than others; test the thickest part of the leg for doneness.

3. Transfer the lamb to a serving board and let it stand for 5 minutes. Slice thin and serve hot.

Makes 10 to 12 Servings

Marinated Grilled Red Pepper Strips

This recipe is perfect for entertaining because it can be prepared a day ahead, perhaps when the grill is already in use.

6 large red bell peppers
¼ cup extra-virgin olive oil
¼ cup white wine vinegar
3 tablespoons freshly squeezed lemon juice
3 cloves garlic, minced
¼ cup minced cilantro
1 tablespoon minced fresh basil *or* **1 teaspoon dried basil**
1 2-ounce can anchovy fillets, drained
¼ cup drained large capers
Fresh basil leaves for garnish (optional)

1. *Grill the Red Peppers:* Using long-handled tongs, grill the peppers over ashen coals for 8 to 10 minutes, until all sides are charred and blistered. Immediately place the peppers in a large plastic bag and secure shut with a twist seal. Let stand for 10 to 12 minutes.

2. Remove the peppers from the bag, cut off the tops, and remove the skins by rubbing gently under cold water. Discard the seeds. Slice the pepper into strips and place the strips in a shallow ceramic dish.

3. *Prepare the Marinade:* Blend the olive oil, vinegar, lemon juice, garlic, cilantro, and basil in a bowl. Drizzle the marinade over the pepper strips. Cover the bowl lightly and refrigerate overnight.

4. At serving time, arrange the pepper strips on a serving plate, place the anchovy fillets decoratively over the peppers, and sprinkle with capers. Garnish with basil leaves if desired.

Makes 6 to 8 Servings

Lamb-Stuffed Zucchini Boats

Today's lamb has a surprise. A 3-ounce lean, cooked serving contains only about 78 milligrams of cholesterol.

Grind your own lean lamb in a food processor. Serve this dish with grilled onion slices and crusty bread.

½ pound lean boneless lamb, cut into 1-inch cubes
1 small onion, minced
½ cup dried bread crumbs
3 tablespoons tomato paste
½ teaspoon ground cumin
¼ teaspoon salt
¼ teaspoon ground cinnamon
⅛ teaspoon red pepper flakes
4 small zucchini
1½ tablespoons freshly grated Parmesan cheese

1. Grind the lamb in a food processor fitted with the steel blade. Place it in a deep bowl and mix in the onion, bread crumbs, tomato paste, cumin, salt, cinnamon, and pepper flakes.

2. Cut the zucchini in half lengthwise. With a teaspoon, scoop out the pulp. Stuff the zucchini boats with the lamb filling, patting the filling firmly into a mound.

3. Prepare the grill for the direct method. When the coals are ashen, replace the oiled grate and place an oiled grill screen over it. Set the zucchini, stuffing side down, on the screen and grill for 1 minute. Turn and sprinkle with cheese. Continue grilling, covered, for 5 minutes or until the zucchini is tender and the lamb done to your taste.

Makes 4 Servings

GAME: VENISON AND BUFFALO

VENISON

Fresh deer meat, or venison, is growing in popularity. From a nutrition standpoint it is an excellent choice. A 3-ounce cooked portion has only 134 calories, less than 3 grams of fat, and 95 milligrams of cholesterol. Venison is extremely rich in iron and other minerals and protein. And as more people discover its distinctive, savory taste, similar to that of lamb, the number of venison ranches increases. Wild deer meat is stronger, with an almost musky flavor.

Be sure that your supplier can vouch for the origin of the venison. It is highly perishable and needs careful handling and constant chilling.

Venison is available in some supermarkets, in specialty meat shops, and by mail order (see Appendix). I have used the most readily available cuts of venison in the recipes that follow.

Versatile venison can be cut into steaks or ground and formed into patties, sausages, and bratwurst that can be grilled. It is well suited to grilling because the intense heat quickly seals the meat. Beware of overcooking, as it loses flavor with each degree of doneness. It's best served with full-bodied or fruit sauces. Enhance the taste tenderness of venison with marinades before grilling. Highly perishable, venison *must* be refrigerated during the marinade process.

BUFFALO

Range feeding promotes lean and healthful meat from buffalo, also called *bison*. A 3-ounce portion of cooked buffalo provides only 122 calories, 2 grams of fat, 70 milligrams of cholesterol, and 24 grams of protein—about half the RDA.

The buffalo is a wild animal, but the meat does not taste at all gamy. Slightly sweet, it has a rich, beefy flavor. Despite its many advantages, buffalo is not widely available, except by mail order. Through the efforts of the National Buffalo Association, that situation is changing, however, and there are now over 400 buffalo producers in the United States.

Trim any visible fat before grilling. Chopped buffalo steak has less fat and water than chopped beef, so it shrinks less. Lean buffalo cooks in less time than lean beef. It is best cooked to rare or medium-rare; well-done buffalo can be tough. Check doneness with a meat thermometer.

Buffalo is delicious smoked. Experiment with some of the sweet woods like apple and cherry.

Blackened Medallions of Venison with Grilled Leeks and Sliced Red Onions

Here's an upscale venison recipe that will impress your cosmopolitan friends. A salad rounds out the meal perfectly.

Mediterranean Marinade (see Index)
4 4-ounce medallions of venison (steak)
1 teaspoon garlic powder
2 tablespoons minced dried onion
½ teaspoon red pepper flakes
½ teaspoon regular chili powder
¼ teaspoon salt
4 to 6 medium leeks, trimmed, washed well, and blanched
1 medium red onion, cut into 4 slices
2 tablespoons extra-virgin olive oil

1. *Marinate the Venison:* Pour the marinade into a large plastic bag and add the venison medallions. Secure the bag shut with a twist seal. Turn the bag so that all surfaces of the venison touch the marinade. Place the bag in a shallow dish and marinate, refrigerated, for 2 to 4 hours.

2. *Prepare the Blackening Spices:* Mix together the garlic powder, dried onion, red pepper flakes, chili powder, and salt in a small dish.

3. *Grill the Venison:* Prepare the grill for the direct method. When the coals are ashen, drain the venison and sprinkle it with the blackening spices. Brush the leeks and onions with the oil. Set the onion slices on the oiled grate and lay a piece of venison over each slice. Grill the venison for 2 to 3 minutes on each side or until done to your taste. The cooking time depends on the thickness of the meat and the distance from the heat source. Venison is best slightly pink on the inside, and it becomes tough when overcooked. Grill the leeks for 2 minutes on each side.

4. Serve venison hot with the leeks and onions.

Makes 4 Servings

Venison Loin with Tangerine Chutney

Venison's natural tang is complemented by peppery seasonings and/or fruits. This chutney combines strong seasonings and fruit. The venison is good with Grilled Fruits (see Index) and Ember-Cooked Potatoes (see Index).

VENISON
Game Marinade (see Index)
1 2- to 3-pound boneless venison loin

TANGERINE CHUTNEY
1 tablespoon canola oil
3 cups chopped onions
2 cloves garlic, minced
⅓ cup sugar
⅓ cup frozen tangerine juice concentrate
1 14-ounce can mandarin oranges, drained
½ cup dark raisins
3 tablespoons chopped candied ginger
¼ teaspoon ground cumin
⅛ teaspoon freshly ground white pepper

1. *Marinate the Venison:* Pour the marinade into a plastic bag and add the venison loin. Secure the bag shut with a twist seal and turn the bag several times to make sure the marinade touches the loin on all sides. Marinate, refrigerated, for 4 to 6 hours or overnight, turning occasionally.

2. *Prepare the Chutney:* Heat the oil in a frying pan. Add the onion and garlic and sauté for 5 minutes over medium heat, stirring often. Stir in the sugar and cook for 15 minutes, or until the onions are golden brown, stirring often. Add the juice concentrate, oranges, raisins, candied ginger, cumin, and pepper. Continue cooking for 1 minute. Spoon the chutney into a bowl. Serve warm.

3. *Grill the Venison:* Prepare the grill for the direct method. When the coals are ashen, drain the venison loin and place it on the oiled grate. Sear by grilling for 1 minute on each side. Continue grilling for about 9 minutes, rotating every 3 minutes; do not overcook (medium is best), or the meat will get tough.

4. Remove the loin to a platter and let it stand for 5 minutes. Meanwhile, reheat the chutney if necessary. Slice the venison thin and serve.

Makes 6 to 8 Servings

Venison Kabobs with Pine Nuts

Serve these kabobs with Ember-Cooked Sweet Potatoes and Jade Green Broccoli Packets (see Index).

TARRAGON MARINADE
3 cloves garlic, minced
¼ cup canola oil
¾ cup tarragon vinegar
¼ teaspoon regular chili powder
¼ teaspoon salt
¼ teaspoon freshly ground pepper

KABOBS
1¼ pounds venison loin, cut into 1-inch cubes
4 10-inch wooden skewers, soaked in cold water for 30 minutes and drained
16 cherry tomatoes
16 pitted large green olives
16 new potatoes, partially cooked
½ cup dried tarragon leaves, soaked in cold water for 10 minutes and drained
½ cup pine nuts

1. *Prepare the Marinade:* Mix the marinade ingredients and pour into a large plastic bag. Set the bag in a bowl and add the venison cubes to the bag. Secure the bag shut with a twist seal and turn the bag several times to make sure all the venison surfaces touch the marinade. Marinate, refrigerated, overnight, turning the bag once or twice.

2. *Grill the Kabobs:* Prepare the grill for the direct method. While the coals are heating, remove the venison from the marinade and thread the skewers with venison, tomatoes, olives, and potatoes. When the coals are ashen, sprinkle them with the tarragon. Place the kabobs on the oiled grate, perpendicular to the grate, or on an oiled grill screen. Grill the kabobs 9 to 12 minutes, rotating every 2 to 3 minutes, until the venison is cooked to your taste. It is best when cooked medium-rare or medium.

3. Arrange the kabobs decoratively on a platter. Sprinkle them with pine nuts.

Makes 4 Servings

Grilled Venison Salad

Grilled Venison Salad comes from friend Liz Clark of Liz Clark's Restaurant, Keokuk, Iowa.

- 4 2-ounce venison filet steaks
- 5 cups mixed salad greens, including some of the stronger greens such as inner leaves of curly endive, radicchio, and arugula
- 4 slices bacon, diced, fried until crisp, and drained
- 4 green spring onions, tops included, minced
- ¼ cup pine nuts, toasted
- 1 avocado, peeled, quartered, and sliced
- 2 tablespoons balsamic vinegar
- ½ cup extra-virgin olive oil
- Coarse sea salt and freshly ground black pepper to taste

1. Prepare the grill for the direct method (or preheat a stove-top grill to 375°F). When the coals are ashen, place the steaks on the oiled grate and grill for 1½ minutes on each side. Remove the steaks from the grill and keep them warm.

2. Toss all salad ingredients in a large bowl, seasoning to taste with sea salt and freshly ground pepper. Place the grilled venison filets flat on a cutting board and, with a sharp knife, slice each filet into strips on the bias. Add the warm venison strips to the salad and toss again. Quickly divide the salad onto four plates and serve while the venison is still warm.

Makes 4 Servings

Venison Steak with Tomato Chutney

Long marinating and quick cooking are the secrets of perfectly grilled venison. These steaks can be cut in half for smaller portions.

GAME MARINADE
¼ cup extra-virgin olive oil
1 cup dry red wine
3 tablespoons freshly squeezed lime juice
2 tablespoons crushed juniper berries
2 scallions, chopped
½ teaspoon dried rosemary

6 ½-inch-thick boneless venison steaks cut
  from the leg, about 6 to 7 ounces each
3 to 4 cups apple twigs, soaked in cold
  water for 30 minutes and drained
Tomato Chutney (recipe follows)

1. *Prepare the Marinade:* Combine all marinade ingredients and pour into a large plastic bag. Add the venison steaks and secure the bag shut with a twist seal. Turn the bag several times to make sure all surfaces of the meat touch the marinade. Marinate, refrigerated, 4 to 6 hours or overnight.

2. *Grill the Venison:* Prepare the grill for the direct method. When the coals are ashen, sprinkle them with the twigs. Drain the venison and place it on the oiled grate. Sear by grilling for 1 minute on each side. Continue grilling for 5 to 6 minutes on each side or until done to your taste. Place on individual plates and serve hot with Tomato Chutney.

Makes 6 Servings

Tomato Chutney

Make extra chutney for gifts or preserve it for later use.

- 4 large tomatoes, peeled and chopped
- 1 large carrot, grated
- 2 large Golden Delicious apples, peeled and cored
- 1 stalk celery, chopped
- 3 tablespoons freshly squeezed lime juice
- 2 slices candied ginger, chopped
- ½ cup cider vinegar
- ¾ cup firmly packed light brown sugar
- ⅓ cup dark raisins
- ¼ cup chopped fresh parsley
- ½ teaspoon ground cinnamon
- ¼ teaspoon ground cloves
- ¼ teaspoon freshly grated nutmeg
- ¼ teaspoon ground allspice

1. Mix all ingredients in a heavy saucepan. Bring the mixture to a boil over medium heat. Reduce the heat and simmer, uncovered, for 1½ hours or until the chutney is thick, stirring frequently.
2. Cool the chutney, place it in a bowl, cover, and refrigerate.

Makes About 3 Cups

Buffalo Rib-Eye Steak with Cilantro Salsa

These buffalo steaks hold their own with the spicy Mexican salsa. Try grilling the steaks over soaked and drained hickory chips. Serve them with jicama salad and Grilled Bananas (see Index).

BUFFALO
Game Marinade (see Index)
4 7- to 8-ounce buffalo rib-eye steaks

CILANTRO SALSA
1 cup roughly chopped cilantro
4 jalapeño chilies, seeded and minced
1 medium onion, minced
1 cup chopped red bell pepper
¼ cup freshly squeezed lime juice
3 cloves garlic, minced
½ teaspoon salt
½ teaspoon ground cumin

1. *Marinate the Buffalo:* Divide the marinade between two large plastic bags. Set the bags in a shallow tray and add two buffalo steaks to each bag. Secure the bags shut with twist seals and turn the bags several times to make sure all buffalo surfaces touch the marinade. Marinate, refrigerated, for 4 to 6 hours, turning the bags occasionally.

2. *Prepare the Salsa:* Toss the salsa ingredients together in a bowl. Let stand at room temperature for 45 minutes to 1 hour.

3. *Grill the Buffalo:* Prepare the grill for the direct method. When the coals are ashen, remove the steaks from the marinade and lay them flat on a large tray. Arrange the steaks on the oiled grill rack and sear by grilling for 1 minute on each side. Continue grilling for 4 to 6 minutes, turn the steaks, and grill for 4 to 5 minutes or until done to your taste.

4. Cut each steak in half and put one serving on each plate. Toss the salsa before passing it at the table.

Makes 8 Servings

WYOMING COWBOY DINNER

Buffalo Burgers with Grilled Onions and Pepper Relish
Venison Steak with Garlic and Shiitake Mushrooms
Baked Beans with a Shot of Whiskey
Cucumber Salad
Two-Onion Bread on the Grill
Watermelon Ice

Buffalo Burgers with Grilled Onions and Pepper Relish

A Griffo-Grill (see Appendix) is a special screen made to fit on an outdoor grill. It is especially helpful when grilling burgers, sausages, fruits, and vegetables because it prevents small pieces of food from falling into the fire.

- 1½ pounds ground buffalo meat cut from the shoulder
- 1 medium onion, minced
- ½ teaspoon salt
- ½ teaspoon garlic powder
- ¼ teaspoon freshly ground black pepper
- 3 cups mesquite chips, soaked in cold water for 30 minutes and drained (optional)
- 2 large red onions, sliced thin into rings
- 2 tablespoons canola oil
- 4 hamburger buns
- **Pepper Relish (recipe follows)**

1. Mix the ground buffalo meat with the onion, salt, garlic powder, and pepper. Divide and form into four patties.

2. Prepare the grill for the direct method. When the coals are ashen, scatter the mesquite chips over them. Replace the oiled grate; use a Griffo-Grill if available.

3. Grill the buffalo burgers, 5 to 6 inches from the heat source, for 1½ minutes on each side or to taste. Brush the onions with the oil and grill for 2 minutes on each side or to taste.

4. Serve the burgers hot with onions, Pepper Relish, and warm buns.

Makes 4 Servings

Pepper Relish

Making relishes was originally a method of preserving vegetables gleaned from the fall harvest. How lucky for us that now we can freeze or can them for future use.

- 1 cucumber, peeled, seeded, and chopped
- 2 large Granny Smith apples, peeled, cored, and minced
- 2 large green tomatoes, chopped
- 1 bunch scallions, chopped
- 1 green bell pepper, seeded and minced
- 2 cups water
- 1 cup sugar
- 1 cup cider vinegar
- 3 tablespoons flour
- 1 teaspoon stone-ground mustard
- 1½ teaspoons salt
- ¼ teaspoon celery salt
- ¼ teaspoon turmeric

1. Combine the cucumber, apples, green tomatoes, scallions, and green pepper in a 1-quart bowl. Cover and refrigerate overnight. Drain any liquid in the bottom of the bowl.

2. Blend the water, sugar, and vinegar in a saucepan. Mix in the vegetables. Bring to a boil over high heat. Combine the flour, mustard, salt, celery salt, and turmeric. Whisk into sugar mixture. Reduce the heat and simmer for 30 minutes, until the mixture thickens, stirring occasionally. Cool.

4. Transfer the relish to a sterilized jar. Cover and refrigerate until needed.

Makes About 8 Cups

Venison Steaks with Garlic and Shiitake Mushrooms

Red wine marinade tenderizes venison and enhances the gamy flavor of the meat.

Red Wine Marinade II (see Index)
4 4- to 5-ounce boneless venison steaks
8 large fresh shiitake mushrooms, stems removed
Canola oil for brushing mushrooms
2 large cloves garlic, sliced thin

1. *Marinate the Venison:* Divide the marinade into two large plastic bags. Set the bags in a bowl and add two venison steaks to each bag. Secure the bags shut with a twist seal and turn the bags several times to make sure all venison surfaces touch the marinade. Marinate, refrigerated, for 4 to 6 hours, turning the bags occasionally.

2. *Prepare the Mushrooms:* Brush the mushroom caps with the oil. Cut two slits in the top of each mushroom. Insert a sliver of garlic into each slit.

3. *Grill the Venison and Mushrooms:* Prepare the grill for the direct method. When the coals are ashen, remove the steaks from the marinade, reserving the marinade, and lay them flat on a large tray. Arrange the steaks on the oiled grill rack and sear by grilling for 1 minute on each side. Continue grilling for 4 to 6 minutes, basting with the marinade. Turn steaks over and continue grilling for 4 to 6 minutes or until done to your taste. I prefer the steaks just pink in the middle. At the same time, grill the mushrooms for about 1 to 2 minutes on each side.

4. Using a spatula or long-handled fork, carefully transfer the steaks to a serving platter. Slice them thin, against the grain, and serve with the grilled mushrooms.

Makes 4 Servings

Baked Beans with a Shot of Whiskey

This recipe can be prepared up to two days before serving time. Remember to discard any shriveled beans. You don't have to soak the beans overnight. The shot of whiskey goes into the beans, not the cook.

- 1 pound dry pinto beans, washed twice and picked over
- 2 tablespoons canola oil
- 3 cloves garlic, minced
- 2 large onions, chopped
- 2 tablespoons bacon-flavored bits
- 2 tomatoes, peeled, seeded, and chopped
- ¼ cup catsup
- ¼ cup molasses
- ¼ cup dark brown sugar
- ¼ teaspoon freshly ground pepper
- ¼ teaspoon ground ginger
- ¾ teaspoon ground cumin
- ¾ teaspoon regular chili powder
- 2 tablespoons prepared mustard
- 1 teaspoon salt
- 2 tablespoons (or to taste) whiskey

1. Put the beans in a large pot and cover them with 3 inches of water. Bring to a boil, reduce the heat, and simmer, covered, until the beans are fork-tender (easily mashed with a fork). Stir occasionally and add more water if necessary. Total cooking time should be about 2½ hours.

2. While the beans are cooking, heat the oil in a frying pan. Add the garlic and onions and sauté for 5 minutes, stirring occasionally. Mix in the bacon-flavored bits.

3. Place the beans in a bean pot or an ovenproof casserole dish. Preheat the oven to 325°F. Blend in the onions, garlic, bacon bits, tomatoes, catsup, molasses, dark brown sugar, pepper, ginger, cumin, chili powder, mustard, and salt.

4. Bake, uncovered, for 2 hours, stirring occasionally. Stir in the whiskey. If you're preparing the beans ahead of time, cool them, cover, and refrigerate.

5. To reheat the beans on the grill, place them in an ovenproof pan or make a packet out of a double layer of aluminum foil. Reheat on the side of the grill grate for 5 minutes, turning the packet occasionally. Or reheat the beans in a preheated 325°F oven for 5 minutes.

Makes 8 Servings

Cucumber Salad

2 large cucumbers
1 large onion, sliced thin
½ cup red wine vinegar
½ cup sugar
1 tablespoon chopped fresh dill
½ teaspoon salt
¼ teaspoon freshly ground pepper

1. Peel the cucumbers and slice them in half lengthwise. Using a spoon, scoop out and discard the seeds. Slice the cucumbers thin and put the slices in a bowl. Toss the cucumbers with the sliced onions.
2. Mix together the remaining ingredients. Toss the dressing with the vegetables. Cover and chill for 3 to 4 hours.
3. When you're ready to serve, toss the ingredients again and place the cucumber salad in individual bowls.

Makes 4 to 6 Servings

Two-Onion Bread on the Grill

This is a versatile side dish that goes well with almost any meat entree. Be creative with toppings, adding other ingredients such as chopped bell peppers, tomatoes, and/or anchovies.

2 eggs, lightly beaten
⅓ cup canola oil
2 cups flour
½ teaspoon salt
¼ teaspoon freshly ground pepper
1½ teaspoons baking powder
2 tablespoons poppy seeds
2 teaspoons honey
¼ cup cold water
3 tablespoons extra-virgin olive oil
4 scallions, minced
2 large onions, minced
2 cloves garlic, minced

1. Using an electric mixer with the dough hook attachment, beat the eggs and oil together. Add the flour, salt, pepper, baking powder, 1 tablespoon of the poppy seeds, the honey, and the water. Mix until the ingredients are combined.

2. Spread the dough evenly into two well-greased large, heavy frying pans or two 9-inch disposable aluminum pie plates. Brush the top of the dough with 1 tablespoon of the olive oil.

3. Heat the remaining olive oil in a frying pan over medium heat. Add the scallions, onions, and garlic and sauté for 4 to 5 minutes, stirring often. Sprinkle the onion mixture and the remaining poppy seeds over the bread dough.

4. Place the frying pan on the grate over waning coals. Cover and grill the bread for 20 minutes. Check to see if it is done after 15 minutes. The top should be golden brown and the bread firm to the touch.

Makes 8 to 10 Servings

Watermelon Ice

Watermelon Ice can be made up to 1 week ahead and kept in a covered container in the freezer.

> **6 cups watermelon pieces, seeds and rind discarded**
> **½ cup superfine sugar**
> **2 tablespoons freshly squeezed lemon juice**

1. Puree the watermelon pieces in two batches in a food processor fitted with the steel blade or in a blender. Mix in the sugar and lemon juice. Pour the puree into a plastic container or an ice cube tray. Cover and freeze until almost set.
2. Process the watermelon ice again in a food processor or blender until smooth.
3. Repeat freezing and pureeing one more time.
4. Cover and freeze for about 3 hours or more, until ready to serve. Leave at room temperature, uncovered, for 5 minutes before serving.

Makes 4 to 6 Servings, About 1 Quart

SMOKED MEATS

SMOKE COOKING

Smoke, the essential ingredient in this grilling method, is produced by adding soaked and drained wood shavings, chips, and twigs to the hot coals. Hickory, mesquite, and apple are the most popular woods. A slight smoke flavor can be obtained on a regular grill by cooking the food with the cover securely in place.

Always buy the smoker that best fits your individual needs. For example, consider the space you have: if your garden is large, you have more options than if you have an apartment balcony. We used a water smoker to test the recipes in this book.

The water smoker, with a pan for water and a pan for the coals as well as a sturdy cover, functions in a slightly different way from conventional grills. The food cooks for a longer time over a slow fire (you should always check the manufacturer's directions for suggested cooking times).

The recipes in this book use no commercially smoked bacon or sausage. Eating only moderate portions of smoked meats no more than several times a week is reasonable to minimize any health-related questions. Remember that this method is a most tasty way of cooking lean meats without added fat, and minimizing fat is a great way to promote health and long-term weight control.

Pork Chops with Winter Fruit Compote

Pork lends itself beautifully to smoking. This recipe yields a moist, delicately flavored, tender meat.

BEER MARINADE
1 12-ounce can beer
3 tablespoons canola oil
¼ cup dark brown sugar
3 bay leaves
¼ teaspoon freshly ground pepper

PORK
6 1-inch-thick pork chops, trimmed of all fat
3 cups cherry or other fruit twigs, soaked in cold water for 30 minutes and drained

Winter Fruit Compote (recipe follows)

1. *Prepare the Marinade:* Combine the marinade ingredients and pour into a large plastic bag. Add the chops and secure the bag shut with a twist seal. Turn the bag several times so that all surfaces of the pork touch the marinade. Place the bag in a flat dish and marinate, refrigerated, for 4 to 6 hours.

2. *Smoke the Pork:* Fill the fuel pan ¾ full of hardwood charcoal and light carefully. When the coals are partially ashen, sprinkle them with the twigs. Fill the water pan ¾ full of hot water. Using pot holders, place the water pan carefully in the smoker. Drain the pork chops and arrange them on the oiled rack in a single layer in the smoker. Cover and smoke for 45 minutes to 1 hour or until all traces of pink are gone. Serve the chops hot with the Winter Fruit Compote.

Makes 6 Servings

Winter Fruit Compote

3 cooking apples, such as Granny Smith, peeled, cored, and sliced
2 cups dried apricots, washed
1 cup seedless grapes, washed
2 cups pitted prunes, washed
½ cup chopped walnuts
1 cup water or apple juice
2 tablespoons honey
½ teaspoon ground cinnamon

1. Mix all ingredients in a medium saucepan. Bring to a boil over medium heat.
2. Reduce the heat and simmer, covered, for 15 minutes, stirring occasionally. Add more water if necessary.
3. Cool completely and ladle into a serving dish. Serve warm or cold.

Makes 6 Servings

Orange-Barbecued Pork Chops

America's Cut™ is a 1½-inch-thick boneless center loin chop with less than ⅛ inch fat and the belly flange removed. Pepper Relish (see Index), chopped onions, and coleslaw made with reduced-calorie mayonnaise make good accompaniments.

ORANGE BARBECUE SAUCE
2 tablespoons canola oil
1 large onion, minced
3 cloves garlic, minced
½ cup prepared chili sauce
¾ cup catsup
2 tomatoes, peeled, seeded, and chopped
¼ cup cider vinegar
⅓ cup freshly squeezed orange juice
¼ cup firmly packed brown sugar
2 teaspoons regular chili powder
½ teaspoon salt
½ teaspoon Worcestershire sauce

PORK
3 6-ounce America's Cut™ pork chops
3 cups mesquite chips, soaked in cold water for 30 minutes and drained (optional)

1. *Prepare the Barbecue Sauce:* Heat the oil in a saucepan. Add the onions and garlic and sauté for 5 minutes, stirring often. Add the remaining sauce ingredients and simmer for 5 minutes, stirring occasionally. Cool the sauce, place it in a covered container, and chill it until needed.

2. *Smoke the Pork:* Fill the fuel pan ¾ full of hardwood charcoal and light carefully. When the coals are ashen, sprinkle them with the mesquite chips. Fill the water pan ¾ full of hot water. Using pot holders, place the water pan carefully in the smoker. Brush both sides of the pork chops with barbecue sauce and arrange the chops in a single layer on the oiled rack closest to the heat source. Cover and smoke for 1 to 1¼ hours or until a meat thermometer registers 160°F. Check for doneness by cutting into meat.

3. Serve hot with barbecue sauce on the side.

Makes 6 Servings

Smoked Tabbouleh-Stuffed Boneless Pork Chops

Tabbouleh is a salad made with bulgur, scallions, and mint. It is Middle Eastern in origin and adapts well to summer cooking. If you have a favorite stuffing and wish to use it instead of tabbouleh, just follow the directions for stuffing the chops and grill. Serve the chops with extra tabbouleh, sliced grilled tomatoes, and black olives.

2 cups cooked bulgur (follow package directions), cooled
⅓ cup extra-virgin olive oil
¼ cup freshly squeezed lemon juice
½ teaspoon salt
½ teaspoon ground allspice
¼ teaspoon ground cinnamon
⅛ teaspoon freshly ground pepper
8 scallions, minced
½ cup minced fresh mint leaves
1½ cups chopped tomatoes
6 ½- to ¾-inch-thick butterflied pork chops, about 5 ounces each, trimmed of all fat
1 tablespoon canola oil
6 tablespoons ground allspice
3 2-foot grapevine cuttings, cut into 6-inch pieces soaked in cold water 30 minutes and drained (see Appendix; optional)

1. Toss the cooled bulgur in a mixing bowl with the olive oil, lemon juice, salt, ½ teaspoon allspice, cinnamon, and pepper. Add the scallions and mint and mix well. Cover the bowl and refrigerate overnight.

2. Pack 2 to 3 tablespoons of tabbouleh stuffing into the center of each pork chop. Close the chop, squeezing the sides together. Brush the outside of each chop with vegetable oil.

3. Fill the fuel pan ¾ full of hardwood charcoal and light carefully. When the coals are ashen sprinkle them with twigs and fill the water pan ¾ full of hot water and add the 6 tablespoons allspice to the pan. Using pot holders, place the water pan in the smoker. Cover and smoke for 1 hour or until done to your taste. After 45 minutes, check the level of fuel and water. Also check the doneness of the chops by cutting in to see color of meat.

4. Arrange the stuffed pork chops on a serving plate and serve hot.

Makes 6 Servings

Hazelnut and Honey Smoked Ham Slices

Be a label reader and shop for the products that are best for you. Some ham slices are lower in fat than others. Look for a lean, well-trimmed ham slice. Serve Spinach Salad with Tarragon Vinegar (recipe follows).

1 8-ounce ham slice, about ¼ inch thick
3 tablespoons honey
½ cup ground hazelnuts
1 orange, sliced

1. Spread both sides of the ham slice with the honey and sprinkle with the ground nuts.

2. Fill the fuel pan ¾ full of hardwood charcoal and light carefully. When the coals are partially ashen, fill the water pan ¾ full of hot water and add orange slices. Using pot holders, place the water pan in the smoker. Arrange the ham slices on the oiled rack closest to the heat source. Cover and smoke the ham for 8 to 10 minutes, turning once.

3. Cut the ham slice into two equal portions and serve hot.

Makes 2 Servings

Spinach Salad with Tarragon Vinegar

1 pound fresh spinach, trimmed, washed, and patted dry
1 8-ounce can water chestnuts, drained
1 large onion, chopped
1 tablespoon Dijon mustard
3 tablespoons tarragon vinegar
½ teaspoon salt
¼ teaspoon freshly ground pepper
¼ teaspoon dried tarragon
¼ cup extra-virgin olive oil
⅓ cup chopped pecans

1. Put the spinach in a salad bowl and toss it with the water chestnuts and onion.
2. In a small bowl, whisk the mustard, vinegar, salt, pepper, and tarragon. Slowly beat in the oil. Add the dressing to the salad and toss.
3. Arrange the salad on six chilled salad plates and sprinkle with chopped pecans.

Makes 6 Servings

Smoked Venison Loin with Raspberry Sauce

Pass crunchy Watermelon Pickles (recipe follows) at the table when you serve this smoked venison.

RASPBERRY SAUCE
- ¼ cup grenadine
- ¼ cup freshly squeezed orange juice
- ¼ cup orange Curaçao or other orange-flavored liqueur
- ¾ cup raspberry vinegar (substitute raspberries in Blueberry Vinegar recipe; see Index)
- ⅓ cup sugar
- ⅛ teaspoon salt
- 1 tablespoon cornstarch, dissolved in 2 tablespoons water
- ½ cup defrosted and drained frozen or fresh raspberries

VENISON
- 3 cups maple twigs, soaked in cold water for 30 minutes and drained (optional)
- 2 pounds boneless venison loin, trimmed of all fat
- 1 tablespoon canola oil
- 2 tablespoons crushed juniper berries

1. *Make the Sauce:* Combine the grenadine, orange juice, Curaçao, raspberry vinegar, 1 tablespoon of the sugar, and the salt in saucepan. Bring the sauce to a simmer over medium heat and continue cooking for 5 minutes, stirring often. While the sauce is simmering, heat the remaining sugar in separate saucepan until golden brown. Carefully, because sauce will spatter, pour the sauce into the heated sugar. Stir in the dissolved cornstarch. Add the raspberries and reduce the heat. Simmer for 2 minutes. Set aside until needed.

2. *Smoke the Venison:* Fill the fuel pan ¾ full of hardwood charcoal and light carefully. When the coals are ashen, sprinkle them with the maple twigs. Fill the water pan ¾ full of hot water and set in the smoker. Brush the venison with the oil and press the juniper berries onto the loin. Place the venison on the oiled grid on the lowest rack. Cover and smoke the venison for about 2 hours, checking it for doneness after 1½ hours. The venison is done when firm and the juices run clear. Replace water and charcoal as needed.

3. Place the venison on a serving platter and let it stand for 5 minutes. Slice thin and serve hot or warm. Pour a thin pool of raspberry sauce onto each plate and arrange the sliced smoked venison on the sauce.

Makes 6 to 8 Servings

Watermelon Pickles

To make a spice packet, use a double thickness of cheesecloth, 3 inches square. Place allspice and cloves in center of cheesecloth. Secure with kitchen string. Discard after using once.

- 2 quarts cubed watermelon rind (¾-inch cubes)
- 3 tablespoons salt
- 2 cups cider vinegar
- 2¼ cups sugar
- 4 cinnamon sticks
- 3 tablespoons chopped candied ginger
- 1 tablespoon whole allspice
- 1 tablespoon whole cloves
- 1 cup water

1. Trim the outer rind from the watermelon, leaving a ¼-inch rim of red watermelon on the rind. Put the watermelon cubes in a large ceramic bowl. Cover with cold water. Mix in the salt, cover, and let stand for 12 to 24 hours. Drain.

2. Rinse the rind and place in a medium saucepan. Cover with water and bring to a boil. Reduce the heat and simmer for 1¼ hours. Drain and cool. Return the rind to a cool saucepan.

3. While the rind is cooking, combine the cider vinegar, sugar, cinnamon sticks, and ginger. Make a spice packet with the allspice and cloves and add it and 1 cup water. Cook over medium heat until the sugar has melted, about 3 to 5 minutes, stirring occasionally.

4. Pour the hot syrup over the drained and cooled rind in the saucepan. Bring to a boil, reduce heat, and simmer over medium heat for 50 minutes. The watermelon rind will be slightly transparent. Cool it, then pour it into a serving bowl, cover, and refrigerate until needed. If desired, watermelon pickles can be packed in hot sterilized jelly jars. Seal according to manufacturer's directions.

Makes 5 to 6 Cups

Hickory-Smoked Strip Steak of Venison

A perfect marriage of flavorful venison, spices, and fruit. The Smoked Eggplant Dipping Sauce takes the place of traditional gravy. Serve with Grilled Zucchini (see Index) and Ember-Cooked Potatoes (see Index).

RED WINE MARINADE II
¼ cup canola oil
1 cup dry red wine
3 tablespoons freshly squeezed lime juice
3 tablespoons crushed juniper berries
2 scallions, chopped
½ teaspoon dried rosemary

VENISON
4 ½-inch-thick strip steaks, about 6 to 7 ounces each
3 to 4 cups hickory chips, soaked in cold water for 30 minutes and drained (optional)
1 cup dry red wine
2 cinnamon sticks

SMOKED EGGPLANT DIPPING SAUCE
1 1½-pound eggplant, cut in half lengthwise
1 tablespoon extra-virgin olive oil
2 cloves garlic, unpeeled
1 cup plain low-fat yogurt
½ teaspoon ground cumin
¼ teaspoon ground allspice
¼ teaspoon ground cinnamon

1. *Prepare the Marinade:* Combine the marinade ingredients and pour into a large plastic bag. Add the venison steaks and secure the bag shut with a twist seal. Turn the bag several times to make sure all surfaces of the meat touch the marinade. Marinate, refrigerated, for 4 to 6 hours or overnight.

2. *Grill the Venison and Eggplant:* Fill the fuel pan ¾ full with hardwood charcoal and light carefully. When the coals are ashen, sprinkle them with the hickory chips. Fill the water pan with ¾ cup hot water, the red wine, and the cinnamon sticks. Using pot holders, place the water pan in the smoker. Arrange the steaks in a single layer on the greased rack closest to the heat source. Brush the cut sides of the eggplant with the olive oil and add the eggplant and garlic to the rack. Cover and smoke for 15 to 20 minutes, until the vegetables are soft. Let the vegetables cool while the venison finishes smoking. Check the fuel, water, and doneness of the meat after 45 minutes. The venison take 45 minutes to 1 hour to smoke.

3. *Prepare the Sauce:* While the venison is smoking, remove the eggplant pulp and spoon it into a bowl. Squeeze the garlic into the bowl and mash to a puree. Mix in the yogurt, cumin, allspice, and cinnamon. Taste the dip to adjust seasonings.

4. Place the sauce in a serving bowl and surround it with cut vegetables such as carrots and celery sticks or warm pita bread triangles. Slice the venison across the grain and place it on individual plates.

Makes 6 Servings of Venison, 6 to 8 Servings (3 Cups) of Sauce

Smoked Strip Loin of Venison with Fresh Coulis of Tomato

This colorful dish is as beautiful to look at as it is to eat. The pasta can be cooked while the venison is smoking and refreshed under hot running water in a strainer before being served.

TOMATO MARINADE
¼ cup canola oil
1 cup dry red wine
⅓ cup tomato juice
½ teaspoon dried marjoram
¼ teaspoon freshly ground pepper

VENISON
1½ pounds venison strip of loin
½ cup dried marjoram, soaked in cold
   water for 10 minutes and drained

FRESH TOMATO COULIS
2 tablespoons extra-virgin olive oil
2 cloves garlic, minced
1 pound (about 3 large) tomatoes, peeled,
   seeded, and chopped
½ teaspoon salt
½ teaspoon dried marjoram
1 teaspoon red wine vinegar
¼ teaspoon freshly ground pepper

ASPARAGUS
½ pound asparagus, trimmed

PASTA
1 pound spinach pasta, cooked according to
   package directions

1. *Prepare the Marinade:* Combine the marinade ingredients and pour into a large plastic bag. Add the venison and secure the bag shut with a twist seal. Turn the bag so all surfaces of the meat touch the marinade. Place the bag on a shallow tray and marinate, refrigerated, for 4 to 6 hours or overnight, turning occasionally.

2. *Prepare the Coulis:* Toss oil, garlic, tomatoes, salt, marjoram, vinegar, and pepper in a bowl. Set aside.

3. *Smoke the Venison and Asparagus:* Fill the fuel pan ¾ full of hardwood charcoal and light carefully. When the coals are partially ashen, sprinkle them with the marjoram. Fill the water pan ¾ full of hot water. Using pot holders, place the water pan in the smoker. Arrange the venison on the oiled rack closest to heat source. Wrap the asparagus in aluminum foil and add it to the rack. Cover and smoke for 20 minutes, then remove the asparagus. Continue smoking the venison for 25 minutes, then check the fuel, water pan, and doneness of the meat. Continue smoking the venison for 15 minutes.

4. Transfer the venison to a platter and let it stand for 5 minutes. Slice the meat into thin strips across the grain. Divide the cooked pasta (refreshed if necessary) onto individual plates. Arrange the venison slices and asparagus spears around the dish. Put a mound of tomato coulis in the center of each plate and serve.

Makes 6 to 7 Servings

Smoked Buffalo Loin Steaks with Kidney Bean Salsa

Serve these smoked steaks with Grilled Corn Pieces (see Index).

BUFFALO
1 tablespoon extra-virgin olive oil
4 6- to 7-ounce boneless buffalo loin steaks
¼ teaspoon garlic powder
3 pieces pecan wood, soaked and drained (optional)

KIDNEY BEAN SALSA
3 tablespoons canola oil
1 large onion, minced
1 large green bell pepper
1 tomato, seeded and chopped
2 tablespoons freshly squeezed orange juice
½ teaspoon salt
½ teaspoon cayenne pepper
2½ cups cooked or drained canned kidney beans

1. *Smoke the Buffalo:* Fill the fuel pan ¾ full of hardwood charcoal and light carefully. When the coals are ashen, add the pecan wood. Fill the water pan ¾ full of hot water. Using pot holders, place the water pan in the smoker. Arrange the steaks in a single layer on the oiled rack closest to the heat source. Cover and smoke for 1 hour. Check the fuel, water pan, and doneness after 45 minutes. The meat is best medium-rare.
2. *Prepare the Salsa:* Combine all salsa ingredients and toss. Set aside.
3. Cut the steaks in half and arrange them on individual plates. Serve with hot or cold kidney bean salsa.

Makes 8 Servings

SAUSAGE AND BURGERS

By making your own sausage and ground meat, you can control the amount of fat in them. Use lean meat cuts or trim the fat before grinding. It's easy to grind slightly frozen cubes of meat in a food processor.

By definition, a sausage is ground meat stuffed into a casing. For ease of preparation, however, none of the recipes in this chapter call for casings. Simply form ground sausage mixtures into the desired shape.

Pork and Veal Burgers on Whole-Wheat Scones

Handle meat as little as possible. It's a good idea to grill burgers on a thin slice of onion or eggplant for an extra flavor boost. Serve these on Whole-Wheat Scones and pass the Champagne Mustard (recipes follow).

½ pound ground veal
½ pound ground pork
1 small onion, minced
½ teaspoon garlic powder
½ teaspoon dried rosemary
½ teaspoon salt
¼ teaspoon freshly ground white pepper

1. Gently mix the ingredients and shape them into four ½-inch-thick patties.
2. Prepare the grill for the direct method. When the coals are ashen, place the burgers on the oiled grate or on an oiled grill screen. Grill, uncovered, for 2 minutes on each side or until done to taste. The burgers will be cooked through yet not overcooked. Place them on individual plates and serve.

Makes 4 Servings

Champagne Mustard

This mustard can also be made with either wine or beer.

> ¼ cup dry mustard
> ½ cup champagne
> ½ teaspoon fennel seeds

Put the mustard in a small bowl. Mix in the champagne and fennel seeds. Let stand for 30 minutes and stir before serving.

Whole-Wheat Scones

> 2 cups unbleached all-purpose flour
> ¾ cup whole-wheat flour
> 1 tablespoon baking powder
> ½ teaspoon salt
> ¼ cup shortening at room temperature
> ¾ cup buttermilk
> 1 egg, slightly beaten
> 1 tablespoon dried crumbled dill

1. Preheat the oven to 450°F. Cover a cookie sheet with aluminum foil or use a nonstick pan.
2. Stir together the flours, baking powder, and salt in the large bowl of an electric mixer. Mix in the shortening. Blend in the buttermilk, egg, and dill.
3. Turn the dough out onto a lightly floured board and knead only until the ingredients are combined. Do not overmix.
4. Roll the dough out ½ inch thick and cut with a 3-inch cookie cutter or glass. Set the scones on the cookie sheet. Rework any remaining dough into scones.
5. Bake for 10 to 12 minutes or until golden brown on top and firm to the touch. Serve warm.

Makes 8 to 10 Scones

Lamb Patties au Poivre with Grilled Parsnips

Use leg of lamb, cut into 1-inch pieces, with all visible fat removed. Grind the lamb in a food processor fitted with the steel blade.

- 1 pound lean ground lamb
- 2 tablespoons cognac
- ½ teaspoon crumbled dried basil
- ¼ teaspoon salt
- 1 tablespoon crushed green peppercorns
- 1 tablespoon crushed white peppercorns
- 8 medium parsnips, cleaned, halved lengthwise, cooked until just fork-tender, and drained
- 2 tablespoons extra-virgin olive oil

1. Mix the ground lamb with the cognac, basil, and salt in a deep bowl. Shape the lamb into four oval patties. Sprinkle the peppercorns over the patties and press them firmly into the meat. Place them on a plate, cover lightly, and chill until ready to grill.

2. Prepare the grill for the direct method. When the coals are ashen, set the lamb patties on the oiled grate or on an oiled grill screen and grill, uncovered, for about 2 to 3 minutes. Turn the patties with a long-handled spatula and grill for another 3 minutes or until done to taste. Lamb is best when just slightly pink in the center.

3. While the lamb patties are grilling, brush the parsnips with the oil and sprinkle with crumbled basil. Grill the parsnips perpendicular to the grate or on an oiled grill screen, at the same time the lamb is grilling, for 2 to 3 minutes on each side or until done to taste.

4. To serve, place the lamb patties on a serving dish, surround them with the parsnips, and serve hot.

Makes 4 Servings

Venison Sausage on Eggplant Slices

When you're making burgers for a crowd, shape the patties ahead of time. Arrange them in a single layer on a tray and freeze them, uncovered, just until the meat is firm. Remove them from the tray and wrap each one securely. Thaw the burgers in the refrigerator before grilling. These sausages are good with spaghetti squash with tomato sauce, Italian bread, and a salad.

1½ pounds boneless venison cut from the shoulder, cut into 1-inch cubes
5 scallions, cut into 1-inch pieces
3 tablespoons brandy
1 egg white
¼ teaspoon ground allspice
¼ teaspoon dried thyme
¼ teaspoon salt
¼ teaspoon freshly ground pepper
1 medium eggplant, cut into 6 lengthwise slices
1 tablespoon extra-virgin olive oil
½ teaspoon dried oregano

1. In two batches, place the venison, scallions, brandy, egg white, allspice, thyme, salt, and pepper in a food processor fitted with the steel blade. Pulse on and off until the meat is ground.

2. Using your hands, roll the venison mixture into six cylindrical sausages about 3 inches by ¾ inch thick. The mixture will be sticky, so keep wetting your hands with cold water while rolling. Brush each slice of eggplant with oil and sprinkle with oregano.

3. Prepare the grill for the direct method. When the coals are ashen, place the eggplant slices on the oiled grate or on an oiled grill screen. Arrange a venison sausage over each slice of eggplant. Grill, uncovered, for 3 minutes, turn, and grill for 2 to 4 minutes or until done.

4. Place a venison sausage and eggplant slice on each of six plates.

Makes 6 Servings

Southwestern Burgers

This recipe turns the ordinary burger on the grill into special party food. Serve with guacamole and gazpacho.

As a general rule, cook burgers over direct heat, using medium-hot coals, and turn them only once. Flattening burgers with a spatula, as we are tempted to do, pushes out valuable juices and leaves the burgers dry.

1¾ pounds regular lean chuck steak or
  "lower-fat" chuck steak, cut into 1-inch pieces
1 small onion, minced
1 teaspoon regular chili powder
½ teaspoon salt
½ teaspoon ground cumin
½ teaspoon garlic powder
⅛ teaspoon cayenne pepper
6 to 8 flour tortillas
2 cups shredded lettuce
2 ripe avocados, peeled and sliced
2 tablespoons freshly squeezed lime juice
1½ cups plain low-fat yogurt
3 cups mesquite chips, soaked in cold water
  for 30 minutes and drained

1. Grind the beef in a food processor fitted with the steel blade, use a meat grinder, or have the butcher grind the meat for you. Place the meat in a deep bowl. Mix in the onion, chili powder, salt, cumin, garlic powder, and cayenne. Shape into seven to eight patties and chill them until ready to grill.

2. Wrap the tortillas in aluminum foil and set aside. Place the lettuce, the avocado drizzled with the lime juice, and the yogurt in individual dishes and set on the table.

3. Prepare the grill for the direct method. When the coals are ashen, sprinkle them with the mesquite chips. Place the burgers on the oiled grate or an oiled grill screen. Grill, uncovered, for 2 minutes, rotate, and grill for 2 minutes longer or until done to taste. The meat should be no more well done than medium. While the burgers are grilling, place the tortillas on the grill to warm them.

4. Place the burgers and warm tortillas on a platter and serve hot. Offer shredded lettuce along with the avocado and yogurt for your guests to top their burgers.

Makes 6 to 8 Servings

Buffalo Burgers Chicago Style

Once buffalo roamed the land in great numbers. By the 1900s they had been so reduced in number that they were very near extinction. We're not sure the buffalo ever roamed in Chicago, but these burgers would be welcome with the traditional Windy City toppings.

1½ pounds boneless buffalo cut from the shoulder, cut into ½- to 1-inch pieces
2 teaspoons dried onion flakes
¼ teaspoon red pepper flakes
3 to 4 cups hickory chips, soaked in cold water for 30 minutes and drained
6 hamburger rolls
½ cup prepared yellow mustard
1 cup sweet pickle relish
1 cup chopped onion
2 large tomatoes, cut into 8 wedges each
16 sport peppers or other hot peppers
2 tablespoons celery salt

1. Grind the meat in a food processor fitted with the steel blade. Mix the ground meat with the dried onion and red pepper flakes. Shape the mixture into six equal patties. Chill until ready to grill.

2. Prepare the grill for the direct method. When the coals are ashen, sprinkle with the hickory chips. Place the buffalo burgers on the oiled grate or on an oiled grill screen and grill, uncovered, for about 2 minutes on each side or to taste. Just before the burgers are cooked, place the rolls on the grill and heat.

3. Place the burgers on the heated rolls. Put the remaining ingredients in individual dishes and allow the guests to garnish their own burgers with them.

Makes 6 Servings

Venison-Stuffed Peppers

Substitute low-fat ingredients for their higher-fat equivalents whenever possible. For example, use reduced-fat sour cream, plain low-fat yogurt, or (in some cases) buttermilk in place of regular sour cream. Ground pork can be substituted for venison. Serve these stuffed peppers with a tossed green salad.

1 pound boneless venison cut from the shoulder, cut into 1-inch pieces
1 whole-wheat pita bread round, crumbled
¼ cup minced fresh parsley
¼ cup buttermilk
¼ teaspoon freshly ground pepper
¼ teaspoon dried marjoram
2 large red or green bell peppers, each one seeded and cut into 4 cuplike pieces

1. Grind the meat in a food processor fitted with the steel blade. Mix the ground meat with the pita crumbs, parsley, buttermilk, pepper, and marjoram. Shape the mixture into eight patties. Set the patties on a plate, cover lightly with plastic wrap, and refrigerate until ready to grill.

2. Prepare the grill for the direct method. When the coals are ashen, pat each venison burger into a pepper "cup" and put them on an oiled grill screen on the grate meat side down. Cover and grill for 2 minutes. Turn and grill until the meat is done to your taste, about 3 to 5 minutes. Serve hot.

Makes 4 Servings

Mexican-Style Sausages on Warm Tortillas

Chorizo is a spicy sausage available in Mexican markets and some large supermarkets. Here's our lean version, made with meat ground at home.

- ¾ pound lean boneless pork, cut into ½- to 1-inch pieces
- 1¼ pounds lean boneless chuck steak, cut into 1-inch pieces
- 3 cloves garlic, chopped
- 1 medium onion, chopped
- 2 tablespoons red wine vinegar
- 3 tablespoons regular chili powder
- 1 teaspoon dried oregano
- 1 teaspoon salt
- ½ teaspoon ground cinnamon
- ¼ teaspoon freshly ground black pepper
- 6 corn tortillas or soft rolls
- 2 cups chopped tomato
- ¼ cup chopped cilantro or parsley

1. Toss the meats, garlic, onion, vinegar, chili powder, oregano, salt, cinnamon, and pepper in a mixing bowl. Put half the sausage mixture into the bowl of a food processor fitted with the steel blade. Pulse about six times or until chopped. Remove the mixture and repeat with the remaining mixture.

2. Put the sausage mixture back in the bowl and cover with plastic wrap. Refrigerate for 4 to 6 hours.

3. Using your hands, shape the sausage into six patties, each about 2½ to 3 inches in diameter and ½ inch thick.

4. Prepare the grill for the direct method. When the coals are ashen, set the sausage patties on the oiled grate or on an oiled grill screen. Grill, uncovered, for 2 minutes. Turn with a long-handled spatula and continue grilling for 2 minutes or until done to your taste. When the sausages are almost cooked, place the tortillas or rolls on the grill to warm them.

5. Place each sausage on a warm corn tortilla or soft roll and sprinkle with chopped tomatoes and cilantro.

Makes 6 Servings

Sausage Salad

Customize a plain burger or sausage with your favorite seasonings. Try basil, marjoram, garlic powder, curry powder, or a blend of chili powder and ground cumin. Do not overcook; most lean meats should not be cooked beyond medium.

1½ pounds boneless lean pork
½ teaspoon ground allspice
½ teaspoon freshly ground black pepper
½ teaspoon salt
⅛ teaspoon ground cloves
4 large cloves garlic, minced
¼ cup skim milk
3 cups washed, dried, and torn arugula
2 tomatoes, sliced
12 pitted black olives
Salt and freshly ground pepper to taste
Freshly grated Parmesan cheese

1. In a large bowl, mix together the pork, allspice, pepper, salt, cloves, garlic, and milk. Divide the mixture into six equal portions and roll each into a sausage ¾ inch thick. Wrap each sausage in plastic wrap, twisting the ends to secure them.

2. Bring 2 quarts water to a boil in a large, deep frying pan. Poach the sausages for 20 minutes. Let them cool, then unwrap them.

3. Prepare the grill for the direct method. When the coals are ashen, replace the grate and set an oiled grill screen over the grate. Grill the sausages on the screen, uncovered, for 1½ to 2 minutes on each side or until done to your taste.

4. Divide the arugula among six salad plates. Slice the hot sausage and arrange the slices over the lettuce. Arrange the tomato slices and olives over the salad. Season with salt, pepper, and Parmesan cheese.

Makes 6 Servings

EMBER COOKING

Ember cooking is just what the term suggests. The food is cooked more by steaming than grilling. Arrange the food, wrapped securely in a double thickness of aluminum foil, on the embers. Turn frequently so that all sides of the food cook evenly.

Individual Osso Buco Packets

Traditionally osso buco is served with risotto, but you can serve spaghetti squash, spaghetti, or a pasta of your choice. Serve Chestnuts Roasted on the Embers (recipe follows) for dessert.

- 4 veal shank bones, cut into 2½-inch-thick pieces, about 1¾ to 2 pounds total
- ½ teaspoon salt
- ½ teaspoon freshly ground pepper
- ¼ teaspoon dried marjoram
- ¼ cup minced fresh parsley
- 2 teaspoons grated lemon zest
- 2 large carrots, sliced thin
- 2 tomatoes, sliced thin
- 4 cloves garlic, minced
- ¼ cup tomato paste
- ¼ cup dry white wine
- ¼ cup chicken broth or veal stock

1. Cut four double thicknesses of aluminum foil large enough to hold equal portions of meat and vegetables. Place them on the counter and arrange equal portions of veal in the center of each. Add the salt, pepper, marjoram, and parsley. Sprinkle with the lemon zest, carrot and tomato slices, and garlic. Dab the top of each veal shank with tomato paste. Begin to fold up the sides of the foil. Sprinkle each shank with wine and broth. Seal the packets.

2. Prepare the grill for the direct method. When the coals are ashen, put the veal packets on the embers. Cover and grill for 35 to 45 minutes, rotating the packets every 15 minutes.

3. Remove one packet to test for doneness. The meat should be tender. Set one packet on each plate and serve hot, allowing guests to open the individual packets.

Makes 4 Servings

Chestnuts Roasted on the Embers

Whole chestnuts can also be roasted on top of the grill (see box). Serve these roasted chestnuts for dessert with a glass of port and grilled pear wedges.

1 pound chestnuts

1. Wash the chestnuts. Using a small, sharp knife, cut a ½-inch X into the top of each chestnut.
2. Cut four or six double thicknesses of aluminum foil into squares large enough to hold the chestnuts. Arrange the chestnuts in the center of each square. Twist the top to seal securely. Cut one ½-inch hole in the side of each package.
3. Prepare the grill for the direct method. When the coals are ashen, place the chestnut packages on the hot coals. Cover and grill for about 40 minutes, rotating the packages every 10 minutes. Remove one package using a pot holder, open the package, and test a chestnut. If not done, replace the chestnut, reseal the package, and continue grilling for 10 minutes.
4. Serve the chestnuts hot or warm. Have guests peel their own chestnuts.

Makes 4 to 6 Servings

TO GRILL CHESTNUTS

Use a chestnut pan or an aluminum pie plate with eight ½-inch holes cut in the bottom. Wash the chestnuts and cut a ½-inch X in the top with a small, sharp knife. Cover the top of the pan with foil. Use a pot holder and shake the pan occasionally. Roast a single layer of chestnuts at a time. Continue grilling until the chestnuts are fork-tender, about 35 to 45 minutes.

Beets in Jackets with Dill Yogurt Sauce

If you like baked potatoes, you'll love beets in jackets.

> 6 medium-large beets, trimmed, leaving 2-inch stem intact
> 2 cups plain low-fat yogurt
> ¼ chopped fresh dill

1. Wash the beets and set each one in the center of a double thickness of aluminum foil large enough to cover it generously, about 12 by 9 inches. Twist the ends to seal securely.
2. Prepare the grill for the direct method. When the coals are ashen, place the beet packets directly on the coals. Cover and grill for 40 minutes, rotating every 15 minutes. The beets are done when fork-tender.
3. While the beets are cooking, mix the yogurt and dill together. Cover and refrigerate until needed.
4. Serve the beets hot. Instruct guests to remove the foil and cut the beets open as they would a baked potato. Spoon the yogurt sauce over the hot beets.

Makes 6 Servings

Veal Stew-Stuffed Pumpkin

Guests receive individual pumpkins, remove the lid, and enjoy the stew in its edible container.

- **2 small pumpkins, each about 5 inches in diameter**
- ½ pound boneless veal stew meat, cut into ½-inch pieces
- ½ cup beef or veal stock
- ¼ cup dry white wine
- ¼ cup chopped onion
- 2 tablespoons chopped fresh parsley
- ¼ cup cooked couscous or rice
- 2 apples, peeled, cored, and chopped
- ¼ cup light raisins
- ½ teaspoon salt
- ½ teaspoon freshly ground pepper
- ½ teaspoon ground cinnamon

1. Remove a 3-inch diameter lid from pumpkin. Scoop out the seeds and threads.
2. In a bowl, toss the remaining ingredients. Divide the mixture between the two pumpkins. Replace the lids.
3. Cut a double thickness of aluminum large enough to hold each pumpkin comfortably and securely. Twist the tops to seal.
4. Prepare the grill for the direct method. When the coals are ashen, set the sealed pumpkins on the embers. Cover and grill for about 1¼ hours, rotating the packets every 20 minutes. To test for doneness, unwrap one packet and see if the meat is cooked. The pumpkins should be cooked but slightly firm. Let guests unwrap their own packets.

Makes 2 Servings

Lamb Shanks with Apricots

The original apricot came from China, and now it is grown in temperate areas in many countries. Most of our apricots are grown in California. Serve the lamb shanks with Grilled Potato Skins (see Index) and Ember-Cooked Sweet Potatoes (recipe follows).

- 4 lamb shanks, each cut in half by butcher, about 2½ to 3 pounds total
- ¼ cup freshly squeezed orange juice or apricot juice
- 2 cups dried apricots
- 8 bay leaves
- ⅓ cup pine nuts
- 1 teaspoon dried marjoram
- ½ teaspoon salt
- ½ teaspoon garlic powder
- ¼ teaspoon freshly ground pepper
- ½ cup dry red wine

1. Cut double thicknesses of aluminum foil into eight 1-foot squares. Set a lamb shank piece in the center of each square. Drizzle with orange juice and sprinkle with apricots, bay leaves, pine nuts, marjoram, salt, garlic powder, pepper, and wine. Twist the foil to seal the packages securely.

2. Prepare the grill for the direct method. When the coals are ashen, place the packages directly on the embers. Cover and grill for 40 minutes, rotating the package every 15 minutes. Remove one lamb package, open, and test for doneness by inserting the tip of a sharp knife into the lamb. The juices should run clear, and the lamb should be just pink in the center.

3. Serve one packet to each guest and allow them to open their own. Discard the bay leaves.

Makes 8 Servings

Ember-Cooked Sweet Potatoes

6 medium sweet potatoes
3 tablespoons reduced-calorie margarine at room temperature
2 teaspoons orange marmalade
12 pistachio nuts, shelled, peeled, and chopped

1. Wash the sweet potatoes and prick each several times with the tines of a fork. Cut six double thicknesses of aluminum foil, each large enough to cover a potato generously. Place a sweet potato in the center of each piece and seal the packets.

2. Prepare the grill for the direct method. When the coals are ashen, arrange the potato packets in the embers, avoiding the edge of the grill. Cover and grill for 40 minutes or until tender, rotating the packets every 15 minutes.

3. While the potatoes are cooking, whisk the margarine in a bowl until fluffy. Beat in the orange marmalade.

4. When the potatoes are cooked, cut a slit in the top of each potato and place a dab of orange "butter" in the center. Sprinkle with pistachio nuts and serve hot.

Makes 6 Servings

Lamb Couscous on the Embers

Couscous is a granular semolina. It is an important part of the North African cuisine. Instant couscous is available at Middle Eastern markets and large supermarkets. Serve with Jade Green Broccoli Packets (recipe follows).

- 2 tablespoons extra-virgin olive oil
- 1 large onion, minced
- 1 large green bell pepper, seeded and chopped
- ½ cup light raisins
- ½ cup sliced almonds
- 1 cup drained canned chick-peas
- ½ teaspoon salt
- ¼ teaspoon freshly ground pepper
- ¼ teaspoon ground mace
- ¼ cup minced fresh parsley
- 3 cups instant couscous
- 1½ pounds boneless lean lamb, cut from the leg into ¾-inch cubes

1. Heat the oil in a frying pan over medium heat. Add the onion and bell pepper and sauté for 4 to 5 minutes, stirring often. Stir in the raisins, almonds, chick-peas, salt, pepper, mace, and parsley. Add 1½ cups water and bring the mixture to a boil. Mix in the couscous and lamb and remove from the heat.

2. Cut a double thickness of aluminum foil about 1 foot square. Line a bowl with the foil so that the foil is pressed against the sides and some foil overhangs the edge of bowl. Pour the couscous mixture into the foil-lined bowl and seal the top securely, using paper clips if necessary.

3. Prepare the grill for the direct method. When the coals are ashen, place the foil packet carefully over the embers. Cover and grill for 15 to 20 minutes, turning the packet on its side after 10 minutes.

4. Place the couscous packet on a plate and take it to the table. Open the packet, being careful of escaping steam. Fluff the couscous with a fork and serve hot.

Makes 6 Servings

Jade Green Broccoli Packets

4 cups broccoli spears, trimmed, cooked until just about fork-tender, and drained
½ cup dark brown sugar
½ teaspoon garlic powder
½ teaspoon ground ginger
¼ cup (or to taste) vodka

1. Cut four 12-inch-square double thicknesses of aluminum foil. Divide the broccoli spears among the centers of the squares. Mix the sugar, garlic, and ginger together. Sprinkle each broccoli packet with the brown sugar mixture and 1 tablespoon vodka. Twist the packets tightly to seal.

2. Prepare the grill for the direct method. When the coals are ashen, put the packets on the embers. Cover and grill for 10 minutes, turning the packets every 3 minutes.

3. Take the broccoli packets to the table and allow guests to open their own steaming packets.

Makes 4 Servings

A GRILL BREAKFAST

Cranberry Spritzers
Breakfast Patties on a Slice of Pineapple
Oatmeal Raisin Muffins
Honey Fruit Kabobs

Cranberry Spritzers

For added flavor, use cranberry juice combinations such as cranberry-raspberry, cranberry-apple, and cranberry-grape.

1 quart cranberry juice
2 cups club soda, chilled
1 cup slightly crushed raspberries (optional)

1. Mix together the cranberry juice and club soda. Pour into individual glasses over ice cubes. Spoon the raspberries over the top of the drink if desired and serve chilled.

Makes 8 Servings

Breakfast Patties on a Slice of Pineapple

1 pound lean ground veal
1 pound lean ground pork
1 cup fine bread crumbs
1 egg white
1 teaspoon dried oregano
1 teaspoon dried sage
1 teaspoon celery salt
½ teaspoon salt
½ teaspoon freshly ground pepper
1 small pineapple, cored, peeled, and sliced thin

1. Combine the veal, pork, bread crumbs, egg white, and seasonings. Shape into eight sausage patties. Refrigerate until ready to grill.

2. Prepare the grill for the direct method. When the coals are ashen, arrange each patty on a slice of pineapple on the oiled grate or an oiled grill screen. Grill, uncovered, for 2 minutes. Turn the patties with a long-handled spatula and continue grilling for 2 to 4 minutes or until done to your taste. Transfer to a platter and serve hot.

Makes 8 Breakfast Patties

Oatmeal Raisin Muffins

1½ cups buttermilk
1¼ cups rolled oats
¼ cup reduced-calorie margarine, melted
½ cup light brown sugar
1 egg
1¼ cups flour
1 teaspoon baking powder
1 teaspoon baking soda
½ cup dark raisins
1 teaspoon vanilla extract
¼ teaspoon freshly grated nutmeg

1. Preheat the oven to 400°F. Put a paper liner in each cup of a 12-cup muffin pan.

2. Mix the buttermilk and oats in a bowl. Let stand for 15 minutes. Blend together the margarine, sugar, and egg. Mix in the oatmeal mixture.

3. Blend in the flour, baking powder, baking soda, raisins, vanilla, and nutmeg just until combined; do not overbeat.

4. Fill each muffin cup ⅔ full of batter. Bake for 20 minutes. Remove muffins from the pan and cool on a rack.

Makes 12 Medium Muffins

Honey Fruit Kabobs

Papayas are grown in semitropical areas. They range in size, and many weigh up to 2 pounds. The flesh is smooth, with both a sweet and sour taste. They are ripe when slightly soft to a firm touch. Papayas are an excellent fruit for grilling.

- 6 10-inch wooden skewers, soaked in cold water for 30 minutes and drained
- 1 small cantaloupe cut into 1-inch chunks
- 1 medium papaya, peeled, seeded, and cut into 1-inch chunks
- 3 large bananas, peeled and cut into 1½-inch pieces
- 3 tablespoons honey at room temperature

1. Using about nine pieces of fruit, thread on each skewer cantaloupe, papaya, and banana. Brush the honey over the fruit.
2. While the breakfast patties are grilling, or just after they have finished grilling, arrange the kabobs on the grill. Cook, uncovered, for 2 minutes, turn over, and grill for 1 to 2 minutes longer.
3. Arrange kabobs on a platter and serve warm.

Makes 6 Servings

Appendix
Mail-Order Sources of Ingredients and Equipment

The Chef's Catalog
3215 Commercial Avenue
Northbrook, IL 60062-1920
(708) 480-9400
Gourmet equipment

Foodstuffs
338 Park Avenue
Glencoe, IL 60022
(708) 835-5105
Gourmet shop, all-purpose

Griffo-Grill
301 Oak Street
Quincy, IL 62301
(217) 222-0700
Grill screens and racks

Holy Land Grocery, Inc.
4806 North Kedzie Avenue
Chicago, IL 60659
(312) 588-3306
Middle Eastern ingredients

Michigan Marketing Association
618 Seymore
Lansing, MI 48933
(517) 371-2411
Dried blueberries, cherries

The Oriental Food Market
2801 West Howard Street
Chicago, IL 60645
(312) 274-2826
Oriental ingredients

People's Gourmet Woods
Don Hysko
55 Mill Street
Cumberland, RI 02864
(401) 725-2700
Pure hardwood charcoal, smoking/cooking woods

Star Market
3349 North Clark Street
Chicago, IL 60659
(312) 572-0599
Japanese ingredients

Wild Game, Inc.
2315 West Huron Street
Chicago, IL 60612
(312) 278-1661
Buffalo, venison

Index

Acorn Squash, Grilled, 29
Alder, as aromatic, 5
Anise-Orange Marinade, 88
Ann Hunt's Top Round with
    Rhubarb-Berry Sauce, 28–29
Apple-Glazed Pork Loin with Green
    Peppercorns, 50–51
Apple–Green Peppercorn Glaze, 50
Apple-Raspberry Sauce, 49
Apples, Grilled, 61
Applewood, as aromatic, 5
Aromatic woods, 4–6
Ash, as aromatic, 5
Asparagus, Grilled, 77
Avocado Salad, 63

Baked Beans with a Shot of Whiskey,
    108–9
Balsamic Vinegar Brushing Sauce,
    32–33
Bananas, Grilled, 65
Barbecue kettle, 3
Barbecue Sauce, 52
    Orange, 114
Barbecue tools, 6
Beef, 13
    Kabobs with Balsamic Vinegar
        Brushing Sauce, 32–33
    rib-eye steak
        grilling guide, 8
        with Five-Herb Sauce, 23
    sirloin steak
        grilling guide, 8
        on Salad with Yogurt
            Horseradish Sauce, 36–37
    Southwestern Burgers, 129
    tenderloin
        grilling guide, 8
        with Chimichurri Brushing
            Sauce, 22
        with Ginger Duxelles, 20–21
    top round
        grilling guide, 8
        with Rhubarb-Berry Sauce,
            Ann Hunt's, 28–29
Beer Marinade, 112–13
Beets in Jackets with Dill Yogurt
    Sauce, 136
Belgian Endive, Grilled, 51
Bell Peppers, Grilled, 81
Black Bean Soup, 62–63
Blackened Medallions of Venison
    with Grilled Leeks and Sliced
    Red Onions, 98
Blueberry and Nectarine Compote,
    Warm, 15

Blueberry Marinade, 28–29
Blueberry Vinegar Dressing, 24–25
Brazier, 3
Bread, Two-Onion, 110
Breakfast Patties on a Slice of
    Pineapple, 142–43
Broccoli Packets, Jade Green, 141
Brushing sauces
    Balsamic Vinegar, 32–33
    Chimichurri, 22
    Hoisin, 56
    Honey-Mustard, 48
    Szechwan Tangerine, 26–27
Buffalo, 97–98
    Burgers Chicago Style, 130
    Burgers with Grilled Onions and
        Pepper Relish, 105–6
    Rib-Eye Steak with Cilantro Salsa,
        104
    Smoked Loin Steak with Kidney
        Bean Salsa, 124
Burgers
    Buffalo Chicago Style, 130
    Pork and Veal on Whole-Wheat
        Scones, 125–26
    Southwestern Beef, 129
Butterflied Leg of Lamb with Potato
    Garlic Sauce, 92–93
Butterflied Leg of Lamb with
    Rosemary Marinade, 94
Butterflied Pork Chops with Sofrito
    Sauce, 42–43

Carpetbag Steak, 14
Champagne Mustard, 126
Charcoal, 4, 10
Cherrywood, as aromatic, 5
Chestnuts, grilling, 135
Chestnuts Roasted on the Embers,
    135

Chimichurri Brushing Sauce, 22
Chuck steak
    grilling guide, 8
    with Szechwan Tangerine Brushing
        Sauce, 26–27
Chutney
    Tangerine, 99
    Tomato, 103
Cider Sauce, 60
Cilantro Salsa, 104
Cinnamon Sauce, 30–31
Citrus Marinade, 46
Cold Grilled Veal with Tuna Sauce,
    80–81
Compote, Nectarine and Blueberry,
    Warm, 15
Corn Pieces, Grilled, 53
Coulis
    Fresh Tomato, 122–23
    Mango, 76
Cranberry Spritzers, 142
Cucumber Salad, 109

Daily food requirements, 1
Direct-heat grilling, 7
Dressing, Walnut Oil, 89
Duxelles, Ginger, 20–21

Easy Veal Loin Chops with
    Blackberries, 77
Electric grill, 3
Electric starter, 5
Ember cooking, 134
Ember-Cooked Potatoes, 17
Ember-Cooked Sweet Potatoes, 139
English Mustard Dipping Sauce, 72

Fig Relish, Spiced, 58
Five-Herb Sauce, 23
Five-Spice Marinade, 47

Flank steak
 grilling guide, 8
 Stuffed, 18–19
 with Tarragon-Almond Sauce, 16
Fruit Compote, Winter, 113
Fruits, Grilled Summer, 79

Garbanzo Beans, Marinated, 83
Gas grill, 3
Ginger and Pepper Vinaigrette, 34–35
Ginger Duxelles, with Beef Tenderloin, 20–21
Glaze, Apple–Green Peppercorn, 50
Grapevine, as aromatic, 5
Green Peppercorn Marinade, 50
Griffo-Grill, 3, 6
Grill basket, 6
Grilled Acorn Squash, 29
Grilled Apples, 61
Grilled Asparagus, 77
Grilled Bananas, 65
Grilled Belgian Endive, 51
Grilled Bell Peppers, 81
Grilled Corn Pieces, 53
Grilled Kiwifruit, 15
Grilled Pineapple, 65
Grilled Potato Skins, 25
Grilled Scallions, 53
Grilled Summer Fruits, 79
Grilled Venison Salad, 101
Grilled Zucchini Spears, 27
Grilling guides, 8–9
Grilling methods, 7–10
Grilling, tools for, 2–3
Ground meat, homemade, 125

Ham
 grilling guide, 9
 Hazelnut and Honey Smoked, 116

Hazelnut and Honey Smoked Ham Slices, 116
Hearts of Palm Salad with Walnut Oil Dressing, 89
Herb Yogurt Sauce, 23
Herb-Tomato Sauce, 38–39
Hibachi grill, 2
Hickory, as aromatic, 5
Hickory-Smoked Strip Steak of Venison, 120–21
Hoisin Marinade and Brushing Sauce, 56
Hoisin-Brushed Pork Tenderloin with Scallion Curls, 56–57
Honey Fruit Kabobs, 144
Honey-Mustard Marinade and Brushing Sauce, 48
Hot Sliced Sirloin Steak on Salad with Yogurt Horseradish Sauce, 36–37
Hungarian Sauce, 70
Hungarian Veal Cutlets, 70

Ices
 Mint, 85
 Watermelon, 111
Indirect-heat grilling, 7
Individual Osso Buco Packets, 134–35
Iowa Double-Cut Pork Chops with Thick Apple-Raspberry Sauce, 48–49

Jade Green Broccoli Packets, 141
Jelly, Two-Pepper, 44–45

Kabobs
 Beef, with Balsamic Vinegar Brushing Sauce, 32–33
 grilling guides, 8–9
 Honey Fruit, 144

Lamb
- Mediterranean, 86–87
- Turkish with Honeydew Wedges, 88–89

Pork
- with Cider Sauce, 60–61
- with Five-Spice Marinade, 47

Tomato, Olive, and Garlic, 82–83

Veal
- and Pork, with Fruit, 78–79
- with Chestnuts and Prunes, 68–69

Venison, with Pine Nuts, 100
Kidney Bean Salsa, 124
Kiwifruit, Grilled, 15

Lamb, 82
- chops
  - with Tomato, Olive, and Garlic Kabobs, 82–83
  - with Thyme, 84
- Couscous on the Embers, 140
- grilling guide, 8
- kabobs
  - Mediterranean, 86–87
  - Turkish, with Honeydew Wedges, 88–89
- leg of lamb
  - with Potato Garlic Sauce, 92–93
  - with Rosemary Marinade, 94
- Mongolian Grill, 90–91
- Patties au Poivre with Grilled Parsnips, 127
- Shanks with Apricots, 138
- Stuffed Zucchini Boats, 96

Leftovers, storing and reheating, 10
Lemon Veal with Pink Pasta, 66–67
Lemon-Sage Marinade, 66–67

Lightly Grilled Steak Carpaccio, 30–31
Lilac, as aromatic, 6
Loin Lamb Chops with Tomato, Olive, and Garlic Kabobs, 82–83
Loin Veal Chops with Garlic and Mushrooms, 74

Mango Coulis, 76
Maple, as aromatic, 5
Marinades, 11–12
- Anise-Orange, 88
- Beer, 112–13
- Blueberry, 28–29
- Citrus, 46
- Five-Spice, 47
- Green Peppercorn, 50
- Hoisin, 56
- Honey-Mustard, 48
- Mediterranean, 86
- Red Wine I, 18–19
- Red Wine II, 120–21
- Rosemary, 94
- Teriyaki, 20–21
- Thai, 54–55
- Tomato, 122–23
- White Wine, 58
- Whole-Grain Mustard, 78

Marinated Garbanzo Beans, 83
Marinated Grilled Red Pepper Strips, 95
Marinated Pork Loin, 64
Meat thermometer, 6, 10
Meat, trimming, 1–2, 7
Mediterranean Lamb Kabobs, 86–87
Mediterranean Marinade, 86
Mesquite, as aromatic, 5
Mexican-Style Sausages on Warm Tortillas, 132

Mint Ice, 85
Mint Salsa, 84
Mixed Greens with Blueberry Vinegar Dressing, 24–25
Mixed Grill with English Mustard Dipping Sauce, 72
Mole Sauce, 40–41
Mongolian Lamb Grill, 90–91
Muffins, Oatmeal Raisin, 143

Nectarine and Blueberry Compote, Warm, 15

Oak, as aromatic, 5
Oakies, as aromatic, 6
Oatmeal Raisin Muffins, 143
Orange Barbecue Sauce, 114
Orange-Barbecued Pork Chops, 114
Osso Buco Packets, Individual, 134–35
Oyster Stuffing, 14

Pasta, Pink, 66–67
Pastry brush, 6
Peanut Sauce, Hot, 54–55
Pecan, 5
Pepper Relish, 106
Peppercorns, crushing, 31
Peppers, Venison-Stuffed, 131
Pickles, Watermelon, 119
Pineapple, Grilled, 65
Pork, 37
   chops
      grilling guide, 9
      Brushed with Two-Pepper Jelly, 44–45
      Butterflied, with Sofrito Sauce, 42–43
      Grilled on Orange Slices, 46
      Orange-Barbecued, 114
      Smoked Tabbouleh-Stuffed, 115
      with Herb-Tomato Sauce and Whole-Wheat Pasta, 38–39
      with Winter Fruit Compote, 112–13
   Ham, Hazelnut and Honey Smoked, 116
   kabobs
      Ribbon Kabobs with Cider Sauce, 60–61
      with Five-Spice Marinade, 47
   loin
      grilling guide, 9
      Apple-Glazed with Green Peppercorns, 50–51
      Marinated, 64
   Satay with Peanut Sauce, 54–55
   tenderloin
      Hoisin-Brushed with Scallion Curls, 56–57
      with Spiced Fig Relish, 58–59
   and Veal Burgers on Whole-Wheat Scones, 125–26
   Virginia-Style Barbecue, 52–53
   with Mole, 40–41
Potato Skins, Grilled, 25
Potatoes, Ember-Cooked, 17
Preserves, Sweet Onion, 73
Protein, 1
Pumpkin, Veal Stew-Stuffed, 137

Raspberry Sauce, 118
Raspberry Whip, 19
Red Cabbage, Sweet and Sour, 59
Red Pepper Strips, Marinated Grilled, 95
Red Wine Marinade I, 18–19

Red Wine Marinade II, 120–21
Red Wine Vinegar Sauce, 75
Relishes
  Pepper, 106
  Spiced Fig, 58
Rhubarb-Berry Sauce, 28–29
Rib-Eye Steak with Five-Herb Sauce, 23
Rosemary Marinade, 94
Rotisserie, 6

Salads
  Avocado, 63
  Cucumber, 109
  Grilled Venison, 101
  Hearts of Palm with Walnut Oil Dressing, 89
  Hot Sliced Sirloin with Yogurt Horseradish Sauce, 36–37
  Mixed Greens with Blueberry Vinegar Dressing, 24–25
  Sausage, 133
  Spinach with Tarragon Vinegar, 117
  Warm Steak, with Ginger and Pepper Vinaigrette, 34–35
Salonika Garlic Sauce, 92
Salsa
  Cilantro, 104
  Kidney Bean, 124
  Mint, 84
Sauces
  Apple-Raspberry, Thick, 49
  Barbecue, 52
  Cider, 60
  Cinnamon, 30–31
  Eggplant Dipping, Smoked, 120–21
  English Mustard Dipping, 72
  Hot Peanut, 54–55
  Hungarian, 70
  Mole, 40–41
  Orange Barbecue, 114
  Raspberry, 118
  Red Wine Vinegar, 75
  Rhubarb-Berry, 28–29
  Salonika Garlic, 92
  Sofrito, 42–43
  Tuna, 80
  Yogurt Beet, 67
Sausage
  homemade, 125
  Mexican-Style on Warm Tortillas, 132
  Salad, 133
  Venison on Eggplant Slices, 128
Scallions, Grilled, 53
Scones, Whole-Wheat, 126
Seaweed, as aromatic, 6
Sirloin Steak, on Salad with Yogurt Horseradish Sauce, 36–37
Skewers, 6
Smoke cooking, 112
Smoked Buffalo Loin Steak with Kidney Bean Salsa, 124
Smoked Eggplant Dipping Sauce, 120–21
Smoked Strip Loin of Venison with Fresh Coulis of Tomato, 122–23
Smoked Tabbouleh-Stuffed Boneless Pork Chops, 115
Smoked Venison Loin with Raspberry Sauce, 118–19
Sofrito Sauce, 42–43
Sorbet, Tequila Lime, 31
Soup, Black Bean, 62–63
Southwestern Burgers, 129
Spinach Salad with Tarragon Vinegar, 117

Starters, 5
Steak Carpaccio, Lightly Grilled, 30–31
Steak, Carpetbag, 14
Stir-frying, 10
Stuffed Flank Steak, 18
Sweet and Sour Red Cabbage, 59
Sweet Onion Preserves, 73
Sweet Potatoes, Ember-Cooked, 139
Szechwan Tangerine Brushing Sauce, 26–27

Tangerine Chutney, 99
Tarragon Vinegar, 17
Tarragon-Almond Sauce, 16
Tequila Lime Sorbet, 31
Teriyaki Marinade, 20–21
Thai Marinade, 54–55
Tomato Chutney, 103
Tomato Coulis, Fresh, 122–23
Tomato Marinade, 122–23
Tomatoes, pureeing, 39
Top Round with Rhubarb-Berry Sauce, Ann Hunt's, 28–29
Tuna Sauce, 80
Turkish Lamb Kabobs with Honeydew Wedges, 88–89
Two-Onion Bread on the Grill, 110
Two-Pepper Jelly, 44–45

Veal, 66
   chops
      with Apples, Onions, and Yogurt, 71
      with Blackberries, 77
      with Garlic and Mushrooms, 74
      with Mango Coulis, 76
      with Red Wine Vinegar Sauce, 75
   Cold Grilled, with Tuna Sauce, 80–81
   Cutlets, Hungarian, 70
   grilling guide, 9
   Individual Osso Buco Packets, 134–35
   Lemon, with Pink Pasta, 66–67
   and Pork Burgers on Whole-Wheat Scones, 125–26
   and Pork Kabobs with Fruit, 78–79
   Ribbon Kabobs with Chestnuts and Prunes, 68–69
   Stew-Stuffed Pumpkin, 137
Venison, 97
   Blackened Medallions with Grilled Leeks and Sliced Red Onions, 98
   Grilled Salad, 101
   Kabobs with Pine Nuts, 100
   loin
      Smoked with Fresh Coulis of Tomato, 122–23
      Smoked with Raspberry Sauce, 118–19
      with Tangerine Chutney, 99
   Sausage on Eggplant Slices, 128
   steak
      Hickory-Smoked, 120–21
      with Garlic and Shiitake Mushrooms, 107
      with Tomato Chutney, 102–3
   Stuffed Peppers, 131
Vinaigrette
   Blueberry, 24–25
   Ginger and Pepper, 34–35
Vinegar
   Blueberry, 24–25

Tarragon, 17
Virginia-Style Barbecue, 52–53

Walnut Oil Dressing, 89
Warm Nectarine and Blueberry Compote, 15
Warm Steak Salad with Ginger and Pepper Vinaigrette, 34–35
Water smoker, 3
Watermelon Ice, 111
Watermelon Pickles, 119
White Wine Marinade, 58

Whole-Grain Mustard Marinade, 78
Whole-Wheat Pasta, with Pork Chops and Herb-Tomato Sauce, 38–39
Whole-Wheat Scones, 126
Winter Fruit Compote, 113

Yogurt Beet Sauce, 67
Yogurt Horseradish Sauce, 36–37

Zucchini Boats, Lamb-Stuffed, 96
Zucchini Spears, Grilled, 27